HATRED

HATRED

The Psychological Descent into Violence

WILLARD GAYLIN, M.D.

PUBLICAFFAIRS
New York

Book design by Jane Raese
Text set in 11 point Berthold Bodoni Antiqua

Library of Congress Cataloging-in-Publication Data
Gaylin, Willard.
Hatred : the psychological descent into violence / Willard Gaylin.
p. cm.
Includes bibliographical references and index.
ISBN 1-58648-166-5
1. Hate. I. Title.
BF575.H3G39 2003
152.4—dc21
2002037139

FIRST EDITION
1 3 5 7 9 10 8 6 4 2

And next to him malicious Envie rode,
Upon a ravenous wolfe, and still did chaw
Between his cankred teeth a venomous tode,
That all the poison ran about his chaw:
But inwardly he chawed his owne maw
At neighbors wealth, that made him ever sad;
For dcath it was, when any good he saw,
And wept, that cause of weeping none he had
But when he heard of harme, he wexed wondrous glad.

EDMUND SPENSER
The Faerie Queene

CONTENTS

CONTENTS

HATRED AS AN ATTACHMENT

THE CULTURES OF HATRED

HATRED

1

CONFRONTING EVIL
HEAD-ON

One day, in July 1941, half of the population of Jedwabne, Poland, murdered the other half—some 1,600 men, women, and children representing all but 7 of the town's Jews. Before killing them, the Poles tortured and humiliated the Jews. They gouged out their eyes with kitchen knives, dismembered them with crude farm instruments, and drowned the women in shallow waters. Infants were pitchforked in front of their mothers and thrown onto burning coals, all accompanied by the shrieks of delight, indeed the laughter, of their neighbors.

The slaughter of the Jedwabne Jews lasted a whole day. And their neighbors, the entire Polish population of the town, either witnessed or participated in the torment. Roughly 50 percent of the adult Polish males were later identified by name as active participants. Even in Nazi Germany whole communities of "normal" people did not rise up to destroy their neighbors. They mostly left that to the professionals while they passively assented—crime enough. In Poland an entire community voluntarily butchered their neighbors and delighted in the activity.

How can one explain such cold passion, such monumental hatred, such cruelty—not on the part of some insane and deranged madman—but by an entire populace in concert, and against the very neighbors who had previously shared their everyday community and life? Jan T. Gross, who wrote an account of the slaughter in his remarkable book, *Neighbors,** made no attempt to explain the phenomenon, having set as his task the meticulous documentation of this seemingly incredible event.

A distinguished journalist, commenting on this book in his column, addressed the question of motivation (always a treacherous and difficult assignment), which Gross chose to ignore. His answer to the question of why the Poles acted with such bestiality and hatred was "because it was permitted. Because they could." This response implies that given the opportunity, we would all delight in such pursuits; thus he denied the special impact of history, culture, religious passion, individual and mass psychology, and paranoia—and blamed it squarely on human nature.

As a lifelong student of human nature and human behavior, I know this to be wrong, dangerously wrong. All of us have the opportunity to torture animals, but the majority of us do not. We are disgusted and bewildered by that minority that takes pleasure in doing so. Surely, then, we would not all avail ourselves of the opportunity to torture our neighbors, given the opportunity. I would not pitchfork an infant merely because the opportunity presented itself ("because it was permitted"), nor would the journalist. I would not pitchfork an infant under duress, nor would he. I would like to think that neither one of us would do it even at risk of our lives, but of this I cannot be sure. And I suspect that the

---

*Jan T. Gross, *Neighbors* (Princeton, N.J.: Princeton University Press, 2001).

columnist himself, when not pressed by journalistic deadlines, would agree that this slaughter was not purely opportunistic.

To say that a massacre such as the one at Jedwabne is not normal to human conduct is obviously not to deny that it is within the stretch of human behavior. *We know that it was done.* But it was beyond normal expectations. A tsunami may occasionally devastate the coast of Japan, drowning thousands, but we do not consider it an expected or reasonable aspect of weather conditions. Human behavior is as unpredictable as, and more variable than, the weather. Such behavior could not have been anticipated by most of us and even now is not believed by many.

Still, while not "natural," hatred is a function of human nature. To understand hatred, one must understand the special qualities of human, and only human, life. Human behavior is famous for its plasticity and variability. As a result, we have witnessed such brothers in humanity as the grotesque Pol Pot and the glorious Saint Francis. Neither of these extremes expresses the expectations one has for ordinary people, but both are testament to the protean nature of the human species. I am not offering these two eccentrics as products of genetic determinism, as I might have with the examples of Newton or Mozart. I am merely acknowledging that conditions can exploit human plasticity to produce unexpected extremes even in relatively normal people. Had I been born in a Palestinian refugee camp and exposed to precisely the same conditions as a suicide bomber, I might have become a suicide bomber. But then again, I might not have. Culture shapes personality, but inheritance is also relevant. Not all of those raised in the camps are prepared to become suicide bombers.

Most animals—from the insect to the higher mammals—have few choices of importance. Everything essential is genetically wired in: how they live, where they live, what they eat, when they mate. This is not true of human beings: We live in tropical islands and arid deserts; in Arctic tundra and equatorial jungles; we control when we have children, if we have children, even how we have children. As a result, the differences among human beings in size, strength, imagination, intelligence, and temperament are unparalleled in the animal kingdom.

Penguins not only look alike, they are alike—not just in our eyes, but in actuality. They possess limited capacity to deviate from their nature. We, in contrast, share with nature in our own design. We were not endowed by nature with wings, but still we fly—and faster than the speed of sound. If a panda cannot find bamboo shoots, he dies. It is bamboo shoots or nothing for him. If we were surviving on bamboo shoots and ran out, we'd eat the panda.

We are more variable because we possess more traits that can be modified; we use our highly developed brains to adapt to the widely diverse environments our imagination drives us to explore. Our lifestyles, conduct, and very physical appearances are so alterable that we might appear to an outside observer as multiple and varied species. This capacity to redesign ourselves, to slip the yoke of instinct and genetics, is a cardinal element of human nature.

The result of this variability is that we are capable of developing into saints or monsters. Still, both of these extremes are alien to the average person leading his ordinary life. Terrorists, sadists, and torturers are the evil examples that define the borders of normal human behavior. We must not trivialize the tragic extremes of their hatred by assuming that they are commonplace representatives of human variability. Such a judgment is an attempt to deny their depravity and contain our anxiety. These people are different from you and me. We are capable of feeling transient extremes of rage that we call hatred, but the true haters live daily with their hatred. Their hatred is a way of life. It is, beyond that, often their raison d'être. They are obsessed with their enemies, attached to them in a paranoid partnership. It is this attachment that defines true hatred.

When we confront the true hater, he frightens us. Too often we struggle to avoid facing this extreme hatred by emotionally distancing ourselves from it. One way to do this is through denial, a mental defense mechanism that permits us to cope in the presence of the unbearable. Its classic embodiment is in the denial of death that is part of the universal human condition. Human beings are burdened with the awareness that their lives must end, independent of anything they may do. We handle the existential dread of death by denying its presence. We go on living as though there were no end. We must do that. We are "in God's hands." It is all part of "a grand design." Our dead child is "safe now," "in a better place."

I do not believe that it is mere coincidence that during a period in which terrorists purposely targeted buses of schoolchildren for maximum effect, the American public embraced a novel like *The Lovely Bones*,* in which dismembered and murdered children are portrayed as living in heaven, sucking lollipops, and playing in fields of flowers in perpetual bloom. We must find ways to avoid facing the abominable and incomprehensible.

Another way of distancing ourselves from horror is by romanticizing it. The right to a "death with dignity" is a recent shibboleth of medical reformers. What they really want is a death without the dying. Not the retching, puking, pained, and bloody death of the intensive care unit, but the romantic death of *Love Story* and *La Traviata*. Of course, we all wish for a "proper" and "dignified" death, but we are unlikely to get it. Dying is rarely dignified, and death is the ultimate indignity. Still we dream of a painless and peaceful death in our sleep, in the comfort of our homes, with the

---

*See Alice Sebold, *The Lovely Bones* (New York: Little, Brown, 2002).

companionship of our loved ones. We create a romantic and rarely achievable illusion. We treat hatred the same way.

A startling and unexpected example of romanticizing an act of hatred appeared in an article in the *New York Times* on April 5, 2002. Unexpected, because it was after 9/11,* and in New York City. The article was entitled "2 Girls, Divided by War, Joined in Carnage." It featured large side-by-side, strikingly similar, pictures of two lovely brunette teenage girls.

"Two high school seniors in jeans with flowing black hair, the teen-age girls walked next to each other up to the entrance of a Jerusalem supermarket last Friday. . . .

"The vastly different trajectories of their lives intersected for one deadly moment, mirroring the intimate conflict of their two peoples. At the door of the supermarket, Ms. Akhras detonated the explosives, killing Ms. Levy and a security guard, along with herself."

The total effect of the article, whether intended or not, was to equate the two in tragedy, like star-crossed lovers drawn to a common cataclysmic end in a romantic movie like *Titanic*. As the article indicates, they were drawn to their deaths via the irony of "two vastly different trajectories." But what distinguished the two was not simply their differing orbits, but their purposes, their reasons for being in that particular grocery store at that particular time. As the article itself succinctly stated: "Ayat al-Akhras, 18, from the Dheisheh refugee camp near Bethlehem, was carrying a bomb. Rachel Levy, 17, from a neighborhood nearby, was carry-

---

*On September 11, 2001, Al Qaeda launched a series of suicide attacks utilizing commercial American airline flights, resulting in the destruction of the World Trade Center buildings in New York City and devastation to the Pentagon in Washington, DC. This caused the loss of thousands of lives. It will be referred to in this text as the 9/11 events, since that is how it is now publicly referred to in the United States.

ing her mother's shopping list for a Sabbath eve dinner." Rachel's purpose was to prepare for celebration of the Sabbath. Ayat's mission was to kill Rachel and as many more of her kind as she could. One was a murderer and the other her victim.

I am not denying the tragedy inherent in the life of the bomber. I admit to being touched by the frustration, the poverty, and the deprivation of the Palestinian refugees. But this story, occurring only seven months after the World Trade Center bombing, indicates the peculiar distortion that remoteness allows, the romanticizing made possible when identification is mitigated by distance. Can anyone imagine the *New York Times* running a similar article with the pictures of Muhammed Atta side by side with a New York City fireman of his age and general appearance? Would the reporter do an extended comparison of their youth and backgrounds, and then describe them as "two young men drawn together by different trajectories," thereby erasing all distinctions between murderer and victim? We want the fireman to be a tragic hero; we do not want to hear of his foibles and imperfections. Muhammed Atta is the identified villain; we are not prepared to hear that he loved dogs and was kind to his mother.

All of us are more capable of distancing ourselves from hatred when we are not bound to the victims in a community of identity. Even in the wake of the World Trade Center bombing, in a city like New York, with great affinities to the Israelis, we do not truly identify with them. They are not of us and we will not "feel their pain" for long. We set different standards for Israeli activities of retribution or self-defense in an assault on the Palestinians than we do for our own pursuit of Al Qaeda in Afghanistan.

We are reluctant—unwilling—to acknowledge and condemn hatred, to confront evil head-on. Evil is the Medusa's head. To see it directly might turn us to stone. So we "rationalize" it. We make it comfortable, by explaining it in everyday terms of sociology and psychology. We look to politics and economics to explain why and how hate-driven acts occur, forgetting that hatred is ultimately a pathological mental mind-set. In such a way we trivialize the acts of terror and in the process romanticize the terrorists, supplying them with ready defenses.

In an article in the *Nation* magazine, Patricia J. Williams bitterly anticipated the eventual distancing from evil in relation to a once-notorious hate crime, the murder of Matthew Shepard, a twenty-one-year-old man who, on October 6, 1998, in Laramie, Wyoming, was severely beaten and then bound to a fence and left to die. Apparently Matthew Shepard was viciously killed only because he was gay.

Williams wrote:

> So here we are, at two minutes after the funeral of Matthew Shepard. The media are awash in earnest condemnation. But mark my words, after three and a half minutes, someone will casually suggest that hatred is just a matter of "ignorance" and "stupidity" and there's no sense in analyzing it too much, because the killers were "just a couple of rednecks." If you're still talking about Matthew Shepard after four minutes, you will be urged to shut up and get on with the healing process. After five minutes, you'll be accused of "magnifying" an isolated misfortune. After six minutes, you will face charges of "exploiting for personal profit what has already been laid to rest."*

Williams is arguing against a moral relativism that has been pervasive in modern culture. Moral relativism denies absolute evil. It abandons strict moral rules, judging behavior in terms of motivation and life history. As a result, we are reluctant to condemn a crime or a criminal. Instead we attempt to "understand" and "treat" the criminal, as we are reluctant to commit what the

---

*Patricia J. Williams, "Canon to the Ordinary, *Nation*, November 9, 1998.

eminent psychiatrist, Karl Menninger, called "the crime of pun-ishment" in the 1950s.* This moral relativism has been sup-ported by a psychoanalytic view of behavior that perceives all present-day behavior as the inevitable—and therefore nonculpa-ble—product of our developmental past. We commit abominable acts because we were conditioned to do so. Since we have no choice, it is not our fault. This reasoning is an imaginative and useful way of treating mental illness in a health setting. I earn my living that way. But it is no way to run a country.

Psychoanalysis erased the formerly rigid distinctions between normal and sick behavior and expanded the definition of mental illness beyond anything imaginable in the nineteenth century. The patients I see in my practice would never have been re-motely identified as having mental health problems a century ago. And that is fine. Fine, that is, in a therapeutic relationship, but not in the world of morality and justice.

Philip Rieff brilliantly labeled this transformation of our cul-ture as *The Triumph of the Therapeutic.*† Illness replaced evil. Nothing was bad, only sick. We became one big, happy therapeu-tic community. The negative implications for the law were signifi-cant when it became clear that if all aberrant behavior were sick, there would be no longer any room for judgment. Therefore, both penance and punishment were outdated. As it turned out, the therapeutic approach to crime and evil was a prelude to disaster, even for the criminals themselves. By calling them sick, we could keep them incarcerated well beyond the sentencing limits that would have been tolerated by law, all in the name of treatment.

One would have thought that the one community that would

---

*Karl Menninger, *The Crime of Punishment* (New York: Viking Press, 1968).

†Philip Rieff, *The Triumph of the Therapeutic: Uses of Faith After Freud* (Chicago: University of Chicago Press, 1987).

resist the conflation of evil into sickness would have been the world of theology. Yet the scandals that erupted in 2002 and plagued the Catholic Church stemmed as much from an abandonment of its moral heritage of distinguishing between good and evil, sinner and saint, and an adoption of the more fashionable language of psychoanalysis, where all aberrant behavior is a sickness requiring treatment.

During the emergence of the scandal involving pederast priests, it was astonishing to read the reports from the Boston archdiocese. The leaders indicated that whereas previously they had viewed sexual offenses of priests in terms of moral transgressions, in the past twenty years or so they were encouraged to adopt a therapeutic approach to the problem. The "problem" being no less than pederasty, lying, violating a position of trust, and desecrating sacred vows.

They were encouraged to adopt a therapeutic approach? By whom? Everyone who had studied the problem had known by then that sexual perversions were intractable to standard—or, for that matter, any—treatments. Never mind that there is no affective treatment for pederasty. Even if there were, that would be the bailiwick of the therapeutic community and we would have preferred the Church to continue its moral fight for righteous behavior.

This abdication by the Church of its traditional role as a moral authority was expressed with numbing clarity by Cardinal Bernard Francis Law, the archbishop of Boston (until late in 2002). In his deposition on his actions in the case of the pedophile priest, the Reverend John J. Geoghan, Cardinal Law stated, "I viewed this as a pathology, as a psychological pathology, as an illness."* He went on to concede that the events had "a

---

*"Excerpts from Cardinal Law's Deposition in a Sex Abuse Suit," *New York Times*, May 9, 2002, p. A36.

moral component," but it was the *illness* that drew his attention and commanded his action. He referred the errant priest to those who better understood this illness, the molester's personal physician and a suspect psychiatrist.

But sick or not, Father Geoghan had violated his vows of celibacy and he had committed multiple homosexual acts viewed by Cardinal Law and his church as grave sins. He had also sodomized innocent children, which is certainly—in addition to being a felony in the Commonwealth of Massachusetts—a sin against God and an act of evil. Surely, violation of vows, corruption of the innocent, sin, and evil fall within the purview and jurisdiction of the Church. Yet these monstrous actions seemed beneath the concern of Cardinal Law, who referred the matter to the attention of his assistants, thus so successfully putting these "incidents" behind him that, when deposed, he was "unable to recall" his most dramatic involvement in these heinous crimes.

I first became aware of this dangerous slippage in the attitudes of the Catholic Church during the 1970s, when I was examining the brutal slaying of a young Yale coed by her fellow student and former boyfriend, Richard Herrin.* The leadership of St. Thomas Moore Church—the seat of the Catholic chaplaincy at Yale—chose to view Herrin, a poor Mexican-American boy from the barrio of Los Angeles, as a victim, more to be pitied than censured. Worse was the tendency of this religious community to "normalize" his behavior by assuming that given the right stimulus, we might all pulverize a loved one's head. Or pitchfork our neighbor's child, I presume.

During an interview I had with Brother Thomas, a Christian Brother in Albany, New York, an incident revealed to me the danger of universalizing, thus normalizing, malignant and even psychopathic and psychotic behavior. The Christian Brothers

---

*Willard Gaylin, *The Killing of Bonnie Garland* (New York: Penguin, 1983).

11

had shielded Richard Herrin when he was on bail in their custody, even allowing this impulsive murderer to attend a college campus under an assumed name. The pedophile shuffle of the Church, revealed only recently, was in full swing during this earlier period, again under the rubric of compassion, understanding, and treatment.

Brother Thomas was the mildest, gentlest of men, with other-worldly qualities that would have made him perfect casting for a thirteenth-century scholastic monk: When I asked him if he could imagine himself ever taking a hammer to the head of a sleeping and innocent girl, the following dialogue occurred, which I record verbatim:

Could you imagine yourself ever taking a hammer and hitting someone?
I could. I could consider that I could not be in control. If something is so outrageous in my makeup that could be triggered and I could just lash out.

Have you ever attacked anyone with an instrument?
No, I haven't.

Yet you have been outraged by social conditions every day of your life.
Yes, I have, but it has been small and inconsequential.

But you really could imagine picking up a hammer and crushing a skull?
I don't know the difference in picking up a hammer and I can see myself losing control and doing practically anything.

Under what conditions have you actually ever lost control?
No, I have never lost control. But I pick up the newspaper and

it seems to happen so much. If it can happen to one person, it can happen to me.

The last naive statement denies the corrupting influence of both family environment and life history. Of course, given the same life history—and even this does a disservice to genetic influences on behavior—we might all do the same thing. But we do not have the same life history, and therefore, we become different people. The adult person who emerged as Saint Theresa and the person who became Agrippina, mother of Nero, were not likely to do the same thing "given the same opportunities."

It is time to reverse the therapeutic trivialization of morality, where nothing is either wrong or right, only sick or healthy. Where nothing is deemed punishable, only treatable. Where evil is only one among other symptoms of mental illness, like depression and anxiety. Where anyone may be excused for any act regardless of how wantonly depraved it is. It is time to liberate morality from the tyranny of psychodynamic models. Even the redoubtable Dr. Menninger became appalled at what he had inadvertently helped to create and in his later days wrote a book entitled *Whatever Became of Sin?**

Most of us are fortunately ignorant of the kind of evil experienced in Jedwabne and the hatred that is the subject of this book. I am not talking about rage, but raw hatred, the hatred that goes beyond betrayal and destruction for purposes of advantage, material gain, or revenge; the hatred that finds pleasure in the pain of others; the hatred of Medea and Iago, of Caligula, Hitler, Pol Pot, and Osama bin Laden. Evidence of such hatred is only too evident in this modern world of tyrants and terrorists, but we have been unready and unwilling to face it. It is time to

---

*Karl Menninger, *Whatever Became of Sin?* (New York: Hawthorn Press, 1973).

confront evil and punish it accordingly. It is time to restore the respectability of moral judgments in public affairs.

Next, we must apply the tools of modern psychological knowledge to the problem of hatred. I do not presume to believe that in the end I, or anyone, will be able to "explain" the Jedwabne massacre. It is incomprehensible. Our minds will not take it in. We cannot recognize such perversity as being explicable within the conditions of human sensibility, any more than we can understand murderers eating the body parts of their victims or men having sex with infants.

Still in this amalgam of malignancy and horror that permeated the Holocaust and the current terrorist attacks, there are common elements of hatred that *are* understandable. A suicide bomb directed at a school bus is composed of the everyday elements of nails, wires, and a cheap radio. It is equally composed of anger, despair, self-justification, cynical manipulation, promise, and perversity. It is time to deconstruct the hater the way we deconstruct his weapons.

"What do they want from us?" is the common question of the day. It is a question that invites socioeconomic and political explanations. But they are insufficient. The question presumes a rational basis for hatred and suggests a direct link between the hater's needs and the selection of his victims. It will not explain the kind of perversity we are today experiencing, any more than it could explain the massacre of the Jews in the Holocaust. It denies the pathological core of hatred. To understand hatred we must do what Euripides and Shakespeare did. We must get into the head of the hater. We now have a psychological framework for doing this. We must apply modern psychological understanding of perception, motivation, and behavior to discover what hatred is. Only when we have identified the nature of the beast can we properly address the environmental conditions that support it.

Hatred is severe psychological disorder. The pathological

haters, whether Al Qaeda today or the Nazis under Hitler, claim to be fighting in defense of an ideology. In truth, the ideology is a convenient rationalization. They are externalizing their internal frustrations and conflicts on a hapless scapegoat population. They are "deluded," and their self-serving and distorted perceptions allow them to justify their acts of hatred against the enemy they have created.

We must start our investigation, therefore, with an examination of the hater's mind rather than his milieu. What is he thinking and feeling? What motivates him? What, if anything, will satisfy him? Does he even know? These are questions that I deal with daily in trying to understand and treat the havoc that the neurotic patient wreaks on himself and those around him. An application of such psychological knowledge is essential if we are to confront the organized terror that now threatens the entire civilized world. To date there has been little call for such information, and little volunteered from the psychological community.

The 9/11 bombings brought home to Americans, in particular, the awareness that understanding hatred is no longer a theoretical problem. We have been treated to pictures of jubilant Arab crowds cavorting in the streets and shouting their delight at the tragic deaths in the United States as a consequence of the World Trade Center massacres. Their palpable hatred of us leaps off the screen, affronting our senses.

There is nothing new about such hatred. What is new is provided by our modern world of technology—the extraordinary reach of the haters and the frightening potential for destruction of the available tools. These innovations add an imperative to the need for containing the emerging cultures of hatred. We must investigate and understand hatred now, before it seeps into our civilized world and destroys our way of life. It is a matter of survival.

2

DEFINING HATRED

Early attempts to define the problem of hatred have not been encouraging. I have already rejected as simplistic (and just plain wrong) the assumption that hatred is normal to the human condition. Even given the opportunity—freedom to do it and go unpunished—we would not all enjoy torturing and killing our neighbors, or even our enemies.

I equally reject the economic and sociological explanations for acts driven by hatred. The desperation in the Palestinian camps does not justify, or explain, the acts of terrorism Palestinians commit. It is not that poverty is irrelevant but that it is not a sufficient condition for hatred; not all poor communities harbor such hatred, nor do they commit terrorist acts. The poverty in America during the Great Depression is incomprehensible to Americans who try to understand it by extrapolation from the "hard times" and recessionary phases of the last thirty years of the twentieth century. The Great Depression was a monumental burden on the American people during the 1930s. Yet there was a remarkable absence of malice toward authority or government. Indeed, the most powerful man in the land, Franklin D.

Roosevelt, was adored by the deprived populations of the country, just as he was abhorred by the privileged classes, who lived in a state of luxury facilitated by the cheap labor of the time.

Nor is poverty a necessary condition for a culture of hatred; not all communities of hatred are poor. The skinheads in America did not arise from any despised and deprived minority. They emerged from the white Protestant community, which constitutes the majority in this country. The lynch mobs in the southern states were culled from the oppressor, not the oppressed, albeit still not the privileged classes in that hierarchical time. The poorest countries of Europe did not sponsor Hitler and the Holocaust. The Germans were hardly the most primitive and uneducated people.

When we began to identify specific terrorists instead of terrorist societies, they confound us by revealing the advantaged nature of their early lives. The Baader Meinhof Gang, which terrorized Germany from 1968 to 1977; Carlos, "the Jackal"; and Kathy Boudin as well as most of her colleagues in the Weather Underground were privileged members of the bourgeoisie. The leaders of Al Qaeda seemed to have emerged largely from the advantaged classes of Saudi Arabia and Egypt. I allow that economic factors are not incidental. They are relevant, but they are not central, as they have been assumed to be. When we do not have answers for social problems, we are likely to assume poverty to be the cause and money the solution. Confessing ignorance, abandoning clichéd and faulty answers, is an essential first step to understanding.

Looking for causes by rounding up the usual suspects, poverty and inequity, will not work here. Worse, it adds two harmful dimensions to the discourse: First, it draws our attention away from a study of the pathological nature of the terrorist. Second, it suggests that if only the victim population had been more charitable, the slaughter would not have occurred—blurring once again the crucial moral distinction between the murderer and the victim, a pervasive tendency in modern liberal cultures. We have behaved like the well-meaning narcissists that we are. We have asked why *they* did this to *us*. We have been searching our souls, when we should have been examining theirs.

The ultimate flaw in the analyses that draw on the history of terrorist populations is that they attempt to locate the root causes of something before defining or even knowing what that something is. To discover the cause of, and thus a cure for, erythroblastosis, one must start with the knowledge that it is a fetal blood disease, not an adolescent skin rash. We must ask what hatred is before we assay the nature of its causes.

Hatred is, if nothing else, a feeling, an emotion. One would logically have expected much of the commentary in response to the 9/11 nightmare in the United States to have focused on human feelings. Instead, the psychology of hatred has barely been mentioned. Having started in the middle of the problem, we are in danger of going off half-cocked. Since the shock of the 9/11 attacks, all sorts of experts have weighed in to explain why this happened. So far no one has called in the doctors.

Because the actions of the terrorists arose in the context of political events, we have concentrated our attentions almost exclusively on historic causes. But before we ask what historic or political factors cause hatred, we ought to ask, "What is hatred?" And that requires a different kind of exploration with a different set of investigative tools. The difference between exploring the causes of an entity and defining its essence leads to a different kind of argument, a different expertise, and is articulated with a different "story line."

The story that emerges with any investigation of human motivation will always vary with the investigative tools employed as well as with the biases of the investigator. A physiologist looking at migraine headache will offer explanations different from those of a psychiatrist. Both will contribute accurate but incomplete knowledge. Each specialist finds answers consonant with her discipline; when your only instrument is a hammer, everything looks like a tack. Looking for the roots, the conditions that created something, directs one inevitably to a historic and political narrative. When, instead of a purely historic event—for example, the rise of fascism in Europe in the 1930s—we are examining a psychological and emotional state like hatred, we had better define the condition before calling in the experts in causation.

Take the example of stress. What causes stress? Where can one locate its roots? Start by defining what one means by stress. There are six distinct and different definitions in my dictionary. If you mean stress as: "an applied force . . . that tends to strain or deform a body,"* and the "body" is a bridge, then one needs to consult an engineer or a metallurgist. On the other hand, if you mean: "a mentally or emotionally disruptive or upsetting condition . . . capable of affecting physical health," you had better call in the doctors. Whether you prefer a psychiatrist or an internist is dependent on your bias. Both would have much to contribute.

Let me make it clear. I am not disparaging historic, sociological, or economic analyses of the roots of hatred. I have learned immeasurably from such sources, but they will not be the focus of this book. They are an essential part of the armamentarium in our battle against the disease of hatred, but they are not alternatives to exploring the nature of hatred. That requires using philosophical and psychological tools. The few great works written in modern times on the nature of hatred have been created by philosophers and psychologists, such as Max Scheler, Gordon Allport, and Jean-Paul Sartre.

---

*All dictionary definitions, unless otherwise specified, are from *The American Heritage Dictionary of the English Language* (New York: Houghton Mifflin, 1992).

The most evident aspect of hatred is the intense emotion that supports it. Therefore, hatred historically was first studied by those interested in human nature and human conduct. In the days before a field of inquiry called psychology existed, human emotion was the purview of philosophy. To understand the influence of emotions on human conduct one turned to the likes of Plato, Aristotle, Bacon, Pascal, Hume, Rousseau, and William James. They were the ones who dissected and examined the complex nature of emotions.

William James was a major transitional figure. With James we see the fusion of the traditional philosophical approach and the burgeoning new field of psychology, in which he was a pioneer. From its earliest days with Freud and Pavlov, psychology has brought a new illumination, a new emphasis, to the analysis of emotions by focusing on the internal psychology, the underlying physiology, and the interpersonal dynamics of the emotions. The emotions are of particular importance when dealing with hatred.

To the average person, hatred is an intense feeling indistinguishable from rage, which it is, if one thinks of hatred only as an emotion. But to leave it at that is to disregard the peculiar complexity of hatred. Hatred is more than an emotion. The *Oxford English Dictionary* gets it exactly right: "Hatred: The condition or state of relations in which one person hates another; the emotion or feeling of hate; active dislike, detestation; enmity, ill-will, malevolence."

This definition places a relationship at the heart of hatred. In this sense, the most precise comparison to hatred would be love. Here, too, the underlying feeling is profound, but it is only part of a unique engagement with another person. We need an object for our hatred or our love. Furthermore, as it would be inappropriate to define an hour or a daylong affinity as "love." It would be equally inaccurate to label an ephemeral feeling of anger toward another as an example of hatred. Both hatred and love must be sustained over a significant period of time to fit the special definitions of these particular relationships. With love, at least, we can use the word "infatuation" to distinguish the rush of the feeling, that instant but fleeting passion, from the complexity of the relationship of love.

We may say we "love" Häagen Dazs ice cream, Louis Armstrong, or gardening, but we do not "love" them, any more than we "hate" brussels sprouts, rap music, or body piercing. The use of love and hate in these situations trivializes the complexities of the hating (and loving) experience. Even when we colloquially use hatred with respect to more-profound ideas, people, or conditions—fascism, drug dealers, child porn—even when we direct hatred toward something that is in itself a serious problem—like bigotry or injustice—these usages of hatred still fall short of the complex definition of hatred I have offered.

Common usages of clinical terms establish a false community. Whenever a woman in the throes of a postpartum depression is tried for the murder of her child, the sympathy and understanding that might be offered her is mitigated by false comparisons. The understanding of her psychosis is adulterated by the fact that everybody in the jury has felt "depressed" at one time or another and they confuse their feelings of depression with the clinical experience. They all know they would not murder their child under the duress of feeling depressed. But like hatred, depression is more than a feeling. As a clinical entity, it bears no relationship to that which we all normally feel when we are blue and "feel depressed." This common usage of the term "depression" diminishes the importance and the unique quality of the pathologic condition. The same is true of hatred. When we assume that at times we feel like a terrorist, we grant the terrorists a normalcy that trivializes a condition that threatens the civilized world.

Because of such usage, most readers will assume that they have experienced hatred, but I know they have not. We are not one with the terrorists. We do not experience that which they feel, nor are we likely to do that which they do. The hatred that requires a defined enemy—the hatred that seeks the humiliation and destruction of that enemy and takes joy in it—is blessedly a rare phenomenon. We must know that we are different from terrorists. In this respect it is imperative to distinguish between the more common feelings of prejudice and bigotry, and that of hatred.

Prejudice and Bigotry

Since many of us are all too aware of signs of prejudice within ourselves, we are often more "understanding" of hate crimes than we ought to be. We equate our prejudices with the hatred of those who commit such crimes. And although prejudice is a way station on the road to hatred, most of us will not travel to the bitter end of that road. What is more, before we can even consider mass hatred—group against group—these various terms must be distinguished, one from the other.

Prejudice is defined in the dictionary as "an adverse judgment or opinion formed beforehand or without knowledge or examination." It means prejudging, not necessarily in a pejorative way. One might have a positive bias. Tell a daughter how beautiful she is or, worse, that she was the prettiest girl at the prom, and her response will be, "Oh, Dad, you're so prejudiced." And she is right. The power of love distorts perception to idealize the subject of our affections. I have a *bias*—"a preference or inclination that inhibits impartial judgment" in relation to those I love.

These days, the term "prejudice" is more often used when the negative attributes ascribed to a person by virtue of his or her being a member of a disdained or despised group are highlighted, or when we voice our feelings toward the pariah group itself. We are always prepared to judge members of such a group severely, and to assume negative behavior or characteristics prior to any evidence. For the purposes of this book, that will be the usage.

It may well be that prejudice against some group, any group—Jews and blacks being historically the most common—is an inevitable consequence of the need to identify with one specific group. I sense this to be true, since almost everyone I encounter exhibits some evidence of prejudice, although I am not yet convinced that in distinguishing "us" from "them" we need to demean "them." The ubiquity of prejudice may be a natural consequence of idealizing one's own. Since the idealization stops at the border of one's family or group, the cold, objective eye reserved for the other perceives his inadequacy in contrast to the idealized version of one's own.

Prejudice actually works toward it. We are likely to expend little emotion on the prejudiced group. We have eliminated those people from our universe of concern. Prejudice often results in a cool indifference—indifference to the sensibilities and even the suffering of those who do not count. Still, the most profound modern statement of the result of racial prejudice in the United States is the Ralph Ellison novel published in 1952 and appropriately titled *The Invisible Man*. Here the protagonist struggles to be *seen*, to become part of the community that seems always oblivious to his needs or his pain.

It should be clear that by distinguishing prejudice from hatred, I am not defining prejudice as less destructive than hatred. Less evil, perhaps, but not less dangerous. The lack of passion and hatred in typical prejudice may contribute to equally great affronts to human dignity. Whereas the hater must demonize the object of its hatred, the prejudiced individual is more likely to dehumanize the object. Slavery, the most iniquitous of human institutions, is a result of such dehumanizing. The slave for the most part was neither loved nor hated. He was chattel at worst. At best, he was treated like a domesticated animal that could be loved as a pet and often more easily disposed of. Slavery demands a violation of that central moral condition, the Kantian imperative never to treat any human being as a means rather than an end. The end result of slavery is as indecent and evil as the cruelty that hatred would produce in the madness of the Holocaust.

Compounding the evil, slavery was accepted by the good citizens in some cultures without shame or apology. Because of this ability to detach the population of the oppressed from membership in the human race, even the most extreme cruelty often went unrecognized. Prejudice turned to hatred in the United States with the liberation of the slaves; when their humanity was reclaimed; when the slaves become a human force; when the fear, if not the guilt, of the white populations was triggered.

For the quintessential statement on how prejudice plays out without hatred one must turn to America's great moral masterpiece, *The Adventures of Huckleberry Finn*. In a scene so brief as to invite being passed over, Mark Twain captured the essence of prejudice.

In a confusing event of mistaken identity that resists replication here, Huck attempts to flimflam kindly and maternal Aunt Sally by passing himself off as Tom Sawyer. In order to explain his delayed arrival he confabulates an explosion aboard a steamboat:

"We blowed out a cylinder head."
"Good gracious! Anybody hurt?"
"No'm. Killed a Nigger."
"Well it's lucky; because sometimes people do get hurt."*

Readers of the novel know that Huck has been on an adventure in which he has risked imprisonment for aiding the runaway

---

*Mark Twain, *The Adventures of Huckleberry Finn* (New York: Signet Classic, 1952), p. 216.

slave, Jim, to gain his freedom. Worse, since Jim is clearly property, Huck believes that in abetting Jim's escape to freedom he is stealing. According to all the grown-ups of his community, Huck's behavior is immoral and un-Christian—a sin as well as a crime. But his love and compassion for Jim overcome his "conscience." Huck shares the prejudices of his day, but in his capacity to love a slave, he demonstrates that he is certainly no bigot.

When one moves from prejudice to "bigotry," one enters the world of the bigot: "one who is strongly partial to one's own group, religion, race, or politics and is intolerant of those who differ." Intolerance suggests an unwillingness to accept the right of the other to be different or to live differently. The bigot will support legislation and social conditions that deprive the minority of its autonomy and its right to be respected. The bigot is prepared to defend a discriminatory environment as extreme as existed in the American South before the civil rights movement or as the apartheid of South Africa until recently. Still, even among members of the Ku Klux Klan, only a minority could participate in burning black children or lynching black men.

Racism may be endemic in white populations, but most whites who embrace it do so with prejudice or bigotry—still short of active hatred. Most racists would not take joy in dragging a chained black man behind the wheels of a truck. They would be appalled. In order to enter into an engagement of hatred, a feeling of being threatened or humiliated by the very presence of the black man as a free member of one's society is essential. The white man must fear the black, must perceive him as a danger. The skinheads among us are such a hating population. They are "attached" to their victims; they are obsessed with them. In saying this, I am not exonerating those who are "only" bigots, for there may be significant slippage between the two groups, that is, those who are bigots and those who are consumed by hatred. Bigotry is a transition point to hatred. Prejudice and bigotry also facilitate the agendas of a hating population. They take advantage of the passivity of the larger community of bigots, a passivity that is essential for that minority who truly hate to carry out their malicious destruction. Even among haters, there will be degrees. There will be those who can torture and kill and those who can only passively approve such actions.

Raul Hilberg, in one of his admirable studies of the Holocaust, drew a distinction between perpetrators and bystanders:

> Most contemporaries of the Jewish catastrophe were neither perpetrators nor victims. Many people, however, saw or heard something of the event. Those of them who lived in Adolf Hitler's Europe would have described themselves, with few exceptions, as bystanders. They were not "involved," not willing to hurt the victims and not wishing to be hurt by the perpetrators. Yet the reality was not so uncomplicated.*

We draw a significant distinction between bigotry and hatred. That distinction is the boundary that separates those who passively observed while the Jews were being slaughtered in the death camps of the Nazis and those who did the slaughtering and enjoyed it. I grant that passivity in the face of evil is a form of moral "activity" and must be held morally accountable. Still, before passing judgment, one must understand what motivated the passivity. It may have been prompted by a lack of courage in those who actually disapproved of the actions. Cowardice is no virtue, but it is still short of evil. On the other hand, it may have been that the bystanders truly enjoyed the suffering. But even here I do not condemn those who only harbor feelings of hatred as much as I condemn those who act on them. The law, and for

---

*Raul Hilberg, *Perpetrators Victims Bystanders: The Jewish Catastrophe, 1933–1945* (New York: HarperPerennial, 1993), p. xi.

the most part the moral law, differentiates between feeling and conduct. Such actions as the torture and murder of the scapegoat population are defining qualities that take us beyond bigotry to hatred.

Some form of prejudice is present in most of us. When evidence of our prejudice surfaces, many of us will, in conscience, feel ashamed. But by the willingness to define our negative attitudes and feelings as "prejudice," we have made a self-critical judgment that mitigates the force and reality of the feeling. A smaller number of us may go beyond prejudice and become actual bigots. With the bigot, the prejudice will not be defined as a failing in himself. The bigot assumes his felt superiority to the alien population is real, not a product of his own pathological viewpoint.

The bigot may have contempt, even disgust, for the outsider, but he will not commit crimes of hatred. A bigot may feel malevolence whenever he thinks of the despised group, but he is not obsessively preoccupied with them. When he becomes so, he crosses the border into hatred. Hatred requires both passion and a preoccupation with the disdained group. It requires an attachment to the hated person or population. And among the population of haters there will be a range of intensity. Many Jew haters among the Nazis who approved of the death camps could not necessarily have performed the acts of destruction. Because of this complexity, hatred can best be understood by exploring its three major components individually:

1. Hatred is clearly and most obviously an emotion, an intense emotion, that is, a passion. To better understand hatred, it is helpful to have some sophisticated understanding of human emotions—the irrational underpinnings of human behavior and the darker side of the human spirit.

2. Hatred is more than an emotion. It is also a psychological condition; a disorder of perception; a form of quasi-delusional thinking. Therefore, to understand the condition of hatred, one must understand the nature of a delusion, a symptom of severe mental disease. One must examine the meaning of the paranoid shift that is central to the thinking of a hating individual and a culture of hatred. This examination will lead us into the somewhat bizarre world of symptom formation.

3. Finally, hatred requires an attachment. Like love, it needs an object. The choice of an object—also like love—may be rational or irrational. Obsessive hatred is by definition irrational. The choice of the victim is more often dictated by the unconscious needs and the personal history of the hater than by the nature, or even the actions, of the hated.

With some understanding of these parts that add up to hatred, we can conceive how much more malignant is the sum of the parts. Since it is the feeling of hatred that directs the terrorist or the bigot to his acts of horror and enables him to justify them in his mind, it seems logical to start our understanding of that which seems beyond understanding—hatred—by examining its emotional underpinnings.

HATRED
AS AN EMOTION

3

RAGE

The Emotional Core of Hatred

For years I have struggled with the task of defining the multitude of human emotions that inform and illuminate the human condition.* Not an easy task. Feelings are not measurable. They have no atomic number or weight. And regardless of how advanced modern biological psychology may become, we are unlikely to find a way to objectively define, calibrate, or titrate an emotion.

It is unlikely that we will ever be able to distinguish such refined emotions as "feeling touched" and "feeling hurt" by analyzing their chemical components. We may never locate the brain centers and neural pathways that differentiate shame from guilt, and even if we do, will that determination advance our under-

---

*The study of emotions has been a major focus of my research and writings, e.g.:, (1) *The Meaning of Despair*; (2) *Feelings: Our Vital Signs*; (3) *The Rage Within: Anger in Modern Life*; and (4) *Rediscovering Love*.

standing of those most subtle of human feelings? To paraphrase the great psychiatrist Franz Alexander, with all the advances expected in the science of acoustics and harmonics, we may someday be able to reduce a Beethoven symphony to frequencies, vibrations, overtones, and so on. But it is inconceivable that we will ever understand the *Eroica* Symphony better that way than by just listening to it.

My definition of the feeling of hatred is as follows: a sustained emotion of rage that occupies an individual through much of his life, allowing him to feel delight in observing or inflicting suffering on the hated one. It is always obsessive and almost always irrational. It has at its core an emotion, albeit one elaborated into a relationship. In everyday life we clarify the meaning of an emotion by saying: "You know how you feel when . . ." The problem with hatred is that most people have never really been part of the experience of hatred, and to make matters worse, they are often confident that they have.

What we can identify with is the underlying feeling of hatred. This is a relatively simple task, since the feeling of hatred is simply an intense form of anger, like rage, something that we have all experienced. Human emotions, like anger, occur in a spectrum of intensity, and we tend to use different words for each step on the scale. Anger starts as annoyance, irritation, or pique and extends to its extremes in rage and fury; it is still all anger. In this text, I will use anger and rage in human beings interchangeably, since both words are used in the literature. With animals, the emotions are less variable in intensity of expression. As a result, in the areas of psychology where animal studies are relevant, the studies tend to refer to the basic emotion as rage. I am inclined to use rage when exploring the biological aspects of hatred.

As we discuss the feeling component of hatred, one must keep in mind that the feeling is only one ingredient in the pathological relationship that defines hatred. Even when we all feel the same, it is still not the same thing. To take a homely example, while the intensity of road rage may astonish us, particularly if we are the ones experiencing it, we are still unlikely to become suicide bombers using our cars to destroy the enemy along with ourselves. The "if I only had a gun" feeling on the highways of America is a metaphoric expression. It does not mean that if we had the gun, we would use it. Those few that would are a pathological minority.

Further, anger is different from hatred by the very ephemeral nature of the feeling. Most of us, even moments later, will not remember the white Pontiac or the man driving it or the fact that he "gave us the finger." After a brief "do you believe that guy?" we will continue our conversation with our passenger right where we left off. Since rage does not compel the paranoid shift associated with hatred, no obsessive involvement is present, no ongoing passionate attachment. The driver of the white Pontiac is not an enemy and will be quickly forgotten.

Aristotle brilliantly distinguished anger from hatred: "Whereas anger arises from offenses against oneself, enmity may arise even without that; we may hate people merely because of what we take to be their character. . . . Moreover, anger can be cured by time; but hatred cannot. . . . And anger is accompanied by pain, hatred is not.*

Pioneering psychologist Gordon Allport, in his monumental book, *The Nature of Prejudice*—close to five hundred pages in the abridged paperback edition—devoted just a brief three pages to the nature of hatred, but he got it right. He clearly distinguished between the various forms of prejudice and hatred. Then drawing on this very discussion in Aristotle, he, too, distinguished hatred from the anger with which it is always associated. He agreed

---

*Aristotle, *Rhetoric*, in *The Basic Works of Aristotle* (New York: Random House, 1941), bk. 2, chap. 4, p. 1389.

that it is the sustained nature of hatred that distinguishes it from the volatile and often passing nature of anger. As he is an interpersonal psychologist, he intuitively latched onto another essential distinction between the two.

Allport stated that anger is an emotion, and by implication purely an emotion, "whereas hatred must be classified as a sentiment—an enduring organization of aggressive impulses toward a person or toward a class of persons."* In other words, the second element of hatred is a profound, if negative, attachment to another person or group. Although Allport did not emphasize or even identify the paranoid shift essential to hatred—he was, after all, a psychologist studying normal personality, not a psychiatrist involved with mental illness—he, nonetheless, came very close: "Since it [hatred] is composed of habitual bitter feeling and accusatory thought, it constitutes a stubborn structure in the mental-emotional life of the individual. By its very nature hatred is extra-punitive, which means that the hater is sure that the fault lies in the object of his hate." This is precisely what Sigmund Freud referred to as "projection" and what I have called the "paranoid shift." Allport continued: "So long as he believes this he will not feel guilty for his uncharitable state of mind."† This absence of guilt, I suspect, is why Aristotle believed that hatred does not involve pain, whereas anger does. But doesn't the person who is exercising an action of righteous rage feel guilt-free, too?

Before elaborating on what distinguishes hatred from anger, it is advantageous to appreciate what they have in common, the emotion. The feeling that is experienced in road rage is fundamentally identical to the feeling in hatred.

---

*Gordon W. Allport, *The Nature of Prejudice* (Garden City, N.Y: Doubleday Anchor Book, 1958), p. 341.

†Ibid.

HATRED

Anger as a Model

Few readers will have experienced hatred as I have defined it. Every reader, without exception, has experienced anger. Since the conditions that elicit anger are the same as those that support hatred, the feeling of anger can be utilized as a stand-in to build a model of hatred.

We all know how feelings color and determine our experiences. We often feel "good" for indefinable reasons; a feeling of joy or well-being needs no analysis or justification. We may, in contrast, find ourselves in a state of anguish or despair for no apparent reason. Here, too, the realistic basis for the shift of feeling may not be all that apparent. Nor for that matter may it be rational. Still, our feelings, not the realities, will determine the quality of our lives—the way we value our existence. The irrational and inappropriate external events that precipitate suicide attempts will horrify the objective observers. More important, when the suicide attempt is unsuccessful, the survivor may, himself, arrive at the same state of bewilderment confronting the trivialities that once convinced him to terminate his life.

Feelings do more than quantify the joy or pain of our everyday life: They also are directives and stimuli, prompting us to specific behavior and responses. Our emotions inform and guide our conduct. As we tend to avoid the sentient experiences of pain and seek pleasure, we listen to our emotions to guide us to sources of pleasure and avoidance of pain. Feelings direct our actions more than we care to admit. We like to think of ourselves as rational animals, but students of human behavior never underestimate the power of the emotional in influencing behavior.

Human beings, both blessed and burdened with an intelligence and a freedom from fixed instinct unparalleled in the animal kingdom, are constantly faced with important choices. Animal lovers insist that animals too must make choices. Whether to eat the mango or the papaya first is of course a choice, but not the kind of significant choice that humans often face. Human beings may decide not to eat anything in the presence of hunger. Despite the drive of intense hunger, they may refuse to eat in order to conserve food for others, or in order to apportion it in an equitable manner, or because they can anticipate a season of want even during a season of plenty. Such anticipation defies other animals, who must always follow the urge of instinct. To help in making such significant choices, human beings are equipped with a repertoire of unique feelings not necessary in other animals, where most of the important decisions are genetically programmed.

Lower animals, with no conscience mechanisms, do not require such emotions as guilt and shame. Guilt and shame are designed to serve our moral values, our better selves. Lower animals do not have "better selves." They are what they are for good and bad, fixed by nature. Fear and rage, however, are emotions common to both the beasts and to us, and we understand their mechanisms better because of the capacity to do animal studies. But the trigger in human beings for either of these emotions differs vastly from that in other animals.

It is impossible to analyze anger without considering it in conjunction with fear. Fear and anger are usually so inextricably intertwined that a psychotherapist is likely to ask a frightened patient what he is angry about, and to ask an angry patient what is frightening him. Fear and rage are generally perceived as the two basic emotions that support our behavior in emergencies. They are part of an elaborate emergency response mechanism built into higher animals. Rage sets in motion the machinery for a frontal physical assault: Appropriate skeletal muscles are tensed; certain muscles are contracted and opposing ones are relaxed; the autonomic system moves to increase the supply of adrenaline and redistribute the blood flow of the body. All of this to prepare the body as an assault weapon.

With fear, the same kinds of physiological responses are initiated, but with opposite distributions of neural stimulation and body chemicals, wiring, and the preparation of different muscles. This time, to facilitate escape. These reactions, wonderfully researched over the years, have come to be called "the fight or flight" responses, after the pioneering work of the American physiologist Walter B. Cannon almost one hundred years ago.* A typical animal experiences these two emotions—and probably only these two—on those occasions when it, its territory, or its breeding rights are under attack. The zebra feels terror with the scent of the lion. He feels rage when the younger male zebra intrudes on his horde.

Most of an animal's time is spent free of emotions. Its "work" is survival, and in that it is guided by rigid instinctual patterns built into its physiology. Food, sex, care of the young, and defense of territory are its sole concerns. Hyenas are not stimulated by imagination of a better life that might be, nor haunted by a sense of inadequacy and deficiency for failing to be better parents or citizens of the community than they are.

Animals survive with the limited resources offered by their biological makeup. They live the same way in the same places doing the same things that their ancestors did eons before. The lamprey inhabits the same ocean depths and is occupied with the same activities that its ancestors did back to the first lamprey of its species. Animals do not imagine the unimaginable. The lion does not aspire to fly like an eagle, roam the seas like a whale, or build "mansions" like termites. Uninspired by imagination,

---

*Walter B. Cannon, *Bodily Changes in Panic, Hunger, Fear and Rage* (New York: Appleton-Century, 1915).

animals do not build ships to explore new worlds, seek new wealth to build new palaces, erect new cities of a grandeur and style inconceivable to their ancestors in the caves. Only Homo sapiens does these things. Only human beings have higher goals and purposes and are equipped with the broad range of feelings that serve this creative imagination. Still, in an emergency, when faced with danger, we will respond with the same basic emotions and physiological responses as the bear and the bobcat.

These emergency emotions of fear and rage were established—biologically fixed through adaptation—into our physiology in those barbaric times that preceded civilized life. For prehistoric people, the meaning and nature of danger were unequivocal. A threat to survival was present. The danger was real and physical—a predatory beast, an enemy horde, a rebellious member of the clan. In these conditions, these emergency emotions served us well. We became an armed instrument for assault. But how about today?

In civilized society—even before the actual threats of terrorists made our culture seem devoid of civilized restraints—we continue to respond to perceived threats with fear and rage. We gear ourselves up for assault. But assault on what? In our civilized existence what dangers remain that are satisfactorily resolved by clubbing? Often it is not the enemy we face, but his agent; more often than not, we are confronted by an idea, a doctrine, or a document—an eviction notice, a dismissal slip, a divorce decree. How does one attack such threats? With one's teeth? We all constantly arm ourselves for dangers that are not physical and cannot be handled via either fight or flight. Worse, some of the threats we perceive exist only in our imaginations.

Once we convince ourselves that the danger is real, we may behave in such a way as to create the very things we contemplate with dread. In either case, the biology set for a prehistoric way of life does not serve us well in the civilized world we now inhabit.

What served the human species so well for the million and a half or more years that we lived in caves has been undone by a mere ten thousand years or so of civilization.

Actual violence still does occur in everyday life, even for twenty-first-century human beings. There is the urban violence of the mugger and his victim; there is the violence in the family where a brutal or drunken man may exercise his rage and frustration on his wife and children, inflicting life-threatening injuries on the helpless. Warlike intertribal battles still occur in some areas. We see it in Africa, where traditional tribes and nations may be confined within artificial geographical borders—Rwanda or Uganda. These hostilities seem always on the verge of erupting into genocidal frenzy. The "tribalism" evidenced in Northern Ireland, central Europe, the Middle East, Africa, and the Indian subcontinent—to name only those areas that made the headlines during the writing of this book—continues to astonish the world.

Notwithstanding the examples culled from the daily newspapers, most fear and rage these days are encountered in situations independent of actual day-to-day events. We read about violence; we do not experience it. Most city dwellers have never been mugged. But in New York until recent times, the amount of conversation about mugging and preparations against it was a testament to how important it was to the psyche of the city dweller. Slights, humiliations, indignities, and disgraces are equally painful even when they involve no physical distress. Worse, the mental disgrace experienced is independent of whether the disrespect is real or imagined. The actual world we live in—except in extremis (hunger, unemployment, war, homelessness, and other privations)—is less important to us than the perceived world. As long as status and power, love and respect, are equated with survival, we may respond to a bad review, a failed job interview, or an admission refusal as a direct assault.

There exists in all humankind a tangled web of feelings that can lead to a sense of failure and despair, a state of helplessness and frustration that can be a halfway station on the road to rage and hatred. These feelings exist in every culture, although the methods of eliciting them will vary. Insecurity is not the exclusive property of any nation or any class. When we enter the symbolic world, as distinguished from the actual and concrete world, there are abundant ways, beyond assault, to feel diminished or endangered. The fact that people suffer from psychological humiliation as profoundly as actual deprivation is a universal truth.

Even when we are faced with true physical danger these days, the nature of that danger and our reaction to it are different than they were in prehistoric times. The danger may come from great distances, from the sky or in a chemically treated letter. Our physiology does not prepare us for these threats. Fight (with whom?) or flight (from whom?) will not work. We are left with a set of built-in biological mechanisms, directives, and signals that will often diminish rather than enhance our chances of survival. Our emergency mechanisms are obsolete.

In an animal, the rage not only prepares it physiologically for the struggle ahead, but also communicates to the opposition its readiness to fight. David Hamburg, a behavioral biologist, describes both the adaptive values and the maladaptive hazards of anger in the following way:

> The angry organism is making an appraisal of his current
> situation, which indicates that his immediate or long-run survival
> needs are jeopardized; his basic interests are threatened.
> Moreover, his appraisal indicates that another organism (or
> group) is responsible for this threat. . . . The tendency is to
> prepare for vigorous action to correct the situation, quite likely
> action directed against the person seen as causing . . . the
> jeopardy. The signals are likely to be transmitted to these

individuals as well as the organism's own decision-making apparatus. The significant others are then likely to respond in a way that will ameliorate the situation.*

This observation continues with an optimism that should be reassuring. Group animals establish a pecking order that serves to avoid constant confrontations. Once in place, this order serves as a civilizing mechanism that facilitates group cohesion and survival. This nice biological mechanism for stabilizing groups has not been as effective in human societies. Most human encounters are not so neatly packaged. Certainly, most of us know better than to attack a policeman or snarl at the boss, but in most social situations the pecking order is not established or, worse, is in a constant state of flux. Too often, the "significant others" will assess the situation differently from the way we do. Their assessment of the pecking order and our relative places in it may differ significantly from ours. Pecking orders in human relationships are rigidly defined only in special groups like the army or the workplace. In social groups they will often be viewed differently by the different participants. And they are ephemeral and readily modifiable. Human beings are often ready to enter the power struggle, to test, challenge, or confront the prevailing order. In human beings the biological imperative to get along with the members of the pack, defined by the pecking order, has been abandoned, without necessarily a different cultural one having been substituted.

The rules are always simpler with lower animals. In animals, aggression is limited for the most part to matters involving food, water, sexual objects, and the territory that commands these.

---

*David Hamburg et al., "Anger and Depression in the Perspective of Behavioral Biology," in *Emotions: Their Parameters and Measurement*, ed. L. Levi (New York: Raven Press, 1975), p. 29.

With human beings, however, what we define as basic interests are usually elaborate, metaphoric, and symbolic, involving such nonbiological factors as status, position, self-esteem, pride, face, and dignity. The cunning human animal is likely to respond to the symbol more aggressively than to the fact. Slights to esteem are weighed with the most delicate of balances, and injuries viewed through the most magnifying of lenses. Human beings appreciate the strength and force of money, the relative power of weapons, the importance of allies and allegiances. And they can check and delay intuitive responses. They can dissemble, anticipate future rectification, store grievances. The human being has a longer perspective. He can anticipate a future and knows that for everything there is a season. He can even bear humiliation while he prepares himself to balance accounts.

Psychiatrists deal on a daily basis with the perceived humiliating aspects of life in our times. Often the symptom that drives the patient to therapy is a persistent and poorly controlled rage or a symbolic equivalent of it. The patient must be guided through this network of conflicting emotions to understand the causes of his diminished sense of self and his tattered ego. This is often a process of tracing the path of a perceived threat that leads to fear, and through fear, to rage. Similarly, to understand those who hate, one must follow the elaborate pathways that lead from vulnerability to hatred.

4

FEELING THREATENED

Fear and anger were designed to serve as responses to threats to our survival. To our survival—not to our pride, status, position, manhood, or dignity. Somehow we have developed in our minds a crucial linkage between even minimally measurable affronts to our status and the very fact of our survival. We respond to these affronts with biological defenses appropriate to an actual assault. Even a simple direct gaze may be perceived as an attack. "Dissing" someone on a subway or the streets of the city may be an invitation to an assault. In the subways of New York City something as inoffensive as a direct look may be interpreted as an act of contempt and assault on dignity.

For years the direct relationship between fear and rage remained undiscovered. Fear was clearly a response to someone who threatened to harm you. Rage was the seemingly opposite emotion. You had rage in the face of someone who affronted you or frustrated you in your pursuits. The intimate connection between them was not appreciated.

These two emotions operate on a toggle switch, readily convertible, one to the other. In cultures where fear is perceived as unmanly—and where is it not?—the emotion of fear is humiliating and must be repressed. Men, real men, do not eat quiche or show fear. Rage is the public face of fear in most men and many women. The two can be considered as opposite sides of the same coin, the same emergency response. Therefore, to determine what enrages a population, look for what threatens them.

Anything in society, in daily life, or in the broader conditions of existence that makes the environment seem more threatening can invoke rage. Anything that diminishes self-confidence or raises questions about one's strength, value, or worth—in other words, one's capacity to defend oneself, one's honor, one's territory—can also invoke rage. The vital balance perceived between the power of "them" and "us"—the measure of our vulnerability—will determine the degree of fear and rage operating on any individual or in a culture.

The unconscious roots of rage are found in all the symbolic ways we feel diminished. Some of the more common psychological assaults perceived by modern people follow. They are often many steps removed from the primal paradigm of the tiger in the compound.

Deprivation

Feeling deprived bears no relationship to the actual amount of comfort or goods that a person may possess. One can be surrounded with all the indulgences of the affluent society and still feel deprived. Contrary to this, we can observe people existing in great poverty, where each expenditure must be measured and considered, every nutrient stored and rationed, who still do not feel deprived.

Human beings can tolerate amazing privation and hardship. People can exist in poverty, even to a point of cold and hunger, with dignity and nobility. I remember as a child watching Robert J. Flaherty's exceptional documentary, *Nanook of the North,* with amazement. I had grown up in the relative comfort of a middle-class family, experiencing little privation, certainly no hunger. Raised in the bleak and extended winters of the Great Lakes, however, I had come to hate the cold.

I watched the Eskimos enduring hunger and poverty, struggling with minimal modern tools to sustain daily life for themselves and their children. Everything depended on the luck of the hunt and the vagaries of nature. The struggle for survival was real here. The hunt was an accepted part of life. Its failure in a season could mean hunger or starvation. Tension and anxiety would be inevitable, but no evidence of self-pity, no sense of "poor me" seemed present in the documentary or was evident in the anthropological studies of these communities.

These lives were lived from birth to death in the bleakest and harshest of environments and in a cold that I could but imagine. Despite hardships that to me would have been unbearable, Nanook and his comrades experienced joy, absolute joy, in their search for food and struggle for survival. In this environment of privation, they not only endured, they triumphed.

During the Great Depression, multitudes suffered true privation and most were not alienated. People were jobless, homeless, and often hungry. Fear was palpable, but not anger. What anger existed focused on the times, the "system," the landlords, and the bosses. The most aberrant response emerged from among the more intellectual-minded who embraced a half-baked and optimistic attraction to Marxist literature and Marxist causes. Although Marxist literature had a peculiar affinity for the hyperbolic language of hatred, most of my socialist relatives and teachers seemed immune to the vitriol and wonderfully free of malice. There was little rage and resentment neighbor to neighbor. All were members of the same community sharing the same fate. I am not trying to romanticize poverty and privation. Grinding poverty is degrading and dispiriting. It is indecent. It can cause severe damage to the spirit and psyche. Only in the capacity to generate rage and hatred is relative deprivation more important than actual privation.

A sense of deprivation thrives on differentials: when others have what we do not. It is a relative feeling, more closely associated with entitlement than want. We suffer from the fact that we do not have that which we need, unless we feel it has—somehow by someone—been denied to us or, worse, taken from us. We then experience a sense of violation, of assault on our dignity that ultimately is perceived as denigration.

When a sense of deprivation ceases to be a transient phenomenon and is perceived as a way of life not just for ourselves but for our group, the parent society is ripe for an explosive release into organized hatred and violence. If this were the Congo in the nineteenth century, such rage could not have been directed at those who actually deprived them. Leopold II, the King of the Belgians, would not even have been known to them and certainly not available. Instead, the resentment might have been deflected onto those who were innocent of cheating them, but in some unfathomable way could have been considered the agents of their deprivation. They might have been a traditional enemy, a neighboring tribe, who by its proximity could afford a convenient outlet for this rage. These local battles became diversions from the true sources of deprivation in the economy or the culture of colonial Africa.

The smoldering rage that results from feeling cheated is always a component of deprivation. Who deprived us is not particularly important. We know deprivation when we see a disparity between that which we have and that which, by observing the standard of some others, we assume to be our due.

Inequity, Unfairness, and Injustice

A sense that the world we occupy operates according to principles of equity and fairness is essential for peace of mind and a relative contentment with the state of authority. The moral sensibility of a child is born within the concept of fairness. "It's not fair" is so often the first statement of moral outrage that one is inclined to believe that some concept of equity or justice must be a part of our genetic inheritance.

Often, this outcry is first heard in the context of sibling rivalry, the sibling "got away with" something, was given something more or better, or was allowed a privilege or indulgence that we were denied. It may be equally present when the parent seems to be changing the rules of the game, violating the standards they, themselves, had previously seemed to endorse. To have played the game according to the rules and still be penalized carries the grievance beyond unfairness to the more generalized feeling of injustice. If the social order is corrupt, outrage and rebellion are justified. This is why the downbeat endings that fascinate so many novelists and movie directors prove to be anathema to the public at large. We want the good guys to triumph and the villains brought to justice. We believe in just deserts.

The anomie that infected some sections of the white working class in the latter half of the twentieth century and led to the various white supremacy movements had its roots in a profound sense of injustice. Members of this group began to feel deceived and treated unfairly (a halfway house to paranoia, as will be discussed later). They felt they had been seduced by promises not kept. They had kept the faith, played by the rules, and still were denied the respect they felt they had earned. The injustice that the bourgeoisie as well as the working class felt may well have started in the 1960s with the revolt of their own children.

The revision of values that began in that decade was perceived by parents as an assault on their standards and way of life. In the short-lived antimaterialism of the student revolt of the 1960s and 1970s, the white middle-class parents joined with the working class in a sense of outrage and betrayal. The parents had purchased the material goods, which their children affected to reject, at extraordinary cost in sweat and labor. They had lived their lives doing unrewarding work, consoling themselves with the assumption that what they could purchase with the earnings from their labors was adequate reward for the sacrifice and drudgery they had endured.

Their children—by rejecting and thereby showing their contempt for split-level homes, two-week vacations, large American-made cars—were challenging the trade-off these parents had been forced to make. Spitting on the flag was not all that outraged these parents; spitting on the twenty-one-inch color television set, the wall-to-wall carpeting, the patio furniture, the microwave oven, and the Buick was worse. Finally, the image of the drop-out child and the druggie became the ultimate assault on the work ethic by which their parents lived—and sacrificed. The children were ridiculing a way of life for which their parents had paid dearly.

In addition, these parents identified the trappings of a middle-class lifestyle as the social sign of their upward progress from the Great Depression days of their childhood. While their children were choosing to go barefoot, they were recalling the times when, for them, going barefoot was not a choice but a necessity. It was a shameful stigma of social caste. For children to affect the dress of the working class—the overalls, the work shoes—was a bewildering rejection of the very status symbols for which the parents had traded much of their pleasure and time. They had sweated out their lives for these "things," not just for their own sake, but for their children's. In attacking these symbols of success, the student revolution had raised doubts about the irrevocable contract that the middle class had signed. It was too painful to acknowledge the possibility that they had opted for simply another mess of pottage.

The social revolution of the late 1960s and the 1970s, with its Nietzschean "reevaluation of values," shook up the working class. To make matters worse, the Great Society, with its rising concern for the rights of minorities, led to welfare programs and affirmative action that seemed to preclude that class. Even worse, the sympathy that the liberal community expressed for the minorities seemed in contrast with the contempt it had for blue-collar tastes and values. White middle- and working-class people were feeling the same injustices that minority groups had been experiencing for years, stemming from the lesser share that they were expected to accept, although for different reasons. They had earned their proper share—not through the "dole" or special consideration, but through their labor and diligence—and now the value of that share was suspect. Somehow or other the promise had been broken. The just rewards for labor had not been meted out. The rules of the game had been changed.

This sense of injustice, of a tacit agreement revoked, continues to feed the mass resentment and rage that led to the many Christian militias formed in the latter half of the twentieth century. The recruits felt that they had paid their dues and had been abandoned and denied by the government they had served in war and peace. They had been betrayed.

Betrayal

The difference between feeling deprived and feeling betrayed is often only a matter of one's identification. We are deprived by "others" who have the power. We are betrayed by our own kind.

The white middle class began to feel deceived and cheated. They had been seduced by promises not kept, and then they were abandoned. They had been "led down the garden path." They had "kept the faith" and had still been "delivered into the hands of the enemy." Worse, they had become the enemy. These feelings and phrases are all part of the language and definitions of betrayal.

We have different expectations of those we love and those we serve than we do of strangers. When those we depend on betray us, we are outraged. Such betrayal will evoke the most fundamental fear of childhood, abandonment by the powerful parental figures.

The fear of being abandoned is compounded by the severe blow to self-esteem that betrayal produces. In life, the indifference and disdain of the impersonal world of strangers is balanced by the concern of those who love us. When that love is trivialized or denied, the balance is dangerously dislocated. If those who we had assumed value us most abandon or discard us, what actual worth can we possess?

A peculiar example of perceived betrayal occurred in the 1930s with the election of Franklin D. Roosevelt to the presidency of the United States. Roosevelt was a member of the elite by every definition. Wealth, religion, and family position marked him as an aristocrat. That is why the egalitarian policies of Roosevelt's New Deal were seen by the wealthy as a stab in the back by one of their own. The wealthy hardly suffered during the depression. If anything, the pool of cheap labor allowed them to maintain their estates and mansions for still another generation. Many historians would later perceive Roosevelt and his policies as being the savior of the capitalist system. Still, the hatred for Roosevelt in the establishment was astonishing in its malevolence and rancor. In a typical display of displacement, the greatest vitriol was reserved for the first lady, Eleanor Roosevelt, a feminist before her time and an uncommon humanitarian. Contempt for ambitious women, an emerging threat to the male oligarchy, added another dimension to their fixation on Eleanor. This was true hatred, as evidenced by their obsession with her and her role in influencing the president's policies. The cruelty extended beyond her actions to her very persona.

Betrayal thus manages to join the fear of rejection with the humiliation of having been deceived. Even when the deceit is a self-inflicted wound based on false assumptions, it will carry with it all the pain and mortification of expectations denied. A betrayed person feels unloved, unsure, and used.

When a significant segment of a society feels betrayed, an environment ripe for anarchy and revolt exists. The rage at the betraying authorities will be compounded by the self-anger one feels for having been accomplice to the deception, for allowing oneself to be duped. The excesses of revolution, the bloodbaths and guillotines, are all testament to the hatred that may be unleashed, particularly if a paranoid element can convince the masses that this betrayal was a calculated humiliation. Germany in the 1930s is a paramount example of a country humiliated, impoverished, and ripe for hatred.

On an individual level, betrayal is most acutely felt in the sexual area. The spurned lover has all the ingredients for hatred at his command. The attachment is there; he need only reverse the emotion from love to hate. Then rage is compounded by the metaphoric meaning of sexuality. For both genders sexuality is a measure of worth and power. Men in our culture—as in most—are taught to see their sexuality as a direct measure of their manhood. Manhood carries the mantle of power. Women, at least traditionally, were taught to view their sexual desirability as the instrument for enlisting the powerful men to aid in their survival. For both men and women, an attack on their sense of sexual worth is a strike at the core of their security. Sexual betrayal can lead to the same viciousness and brutality one sees in suicide bombers. When a body is discovered with a single blow to the head or a single stab wound, an intruder or a stranger may be suspected. When there are twenty or thirty blows, one is likely to be dealing with a frustrated or spurned lover.

Exploitation and Manipulation

Disapproval, deprivation, and betrayal exploit our inner feelings of inadequacy. Unsure of our own capacities, we feel our survival threatened when the value and esteem in which we are held by powerful authority figures or their representatives are brought into question. There are, in addition, direct assaults on our self-worth, direct affronts to pride and confidence. Exploitation and manipulation deprive us of the special status inherent in being a human being. When we feel "used," we feel our very personhood is assaulted.

The ultimate, rawest, and most outrageous use of people is found in the institution of slavery, which is why it is universally condemned in theory if not in practice. In slavery the person is stripped of all rights of humanity and converted into a machine. But to be used in any sense is to violate that basic imperative of moral behavior set down by Immanuel Kant as at the heart of his ethics: Never use a person as a means rather than an end, for in so doing you erase the distinction between person and thing.

We go through life exposed to a continuum of circumstances in which we can never be sure whether we are valued for our services or for ourselves. Since our services are inextricably bound to that which we call our "self," a direct request for services can often be seen as honoring that which we can do and, therefore, that which we are. When lying and deceit are involved, we know that we have been manipulated, used as a means to someone else's end. This explains our anger in the face of even well-intended manipulation. Paternalism is one example of this. Paternalistic medicine, even when practiced for reasons of compassion, came to be resented during the latter half of the twentieth century. When physicians attempted to shield patients from the most malignant implications of their diseases, the patients felt "patronized" and took offense. Truth telling took priority over beneficence. Patients implore doctors to give them the unvarnished truth, but most will resent it if a doctor responds by telling them that they have an incurable cancer.

Still, doctors should honor the truth, while trying to offer some latitude for hope and comfort. When we try to control or influence our patients by means that bypass their rationality, will, and volition, we diminish their autonomy. We reduce them. When they sense this, they will respond with rage.

Frustration

Anyone or anything that makes us feel less whole, less powerful, less useful, and less valued will make us feel endangered. We depend on others and the respect of others to support our self-esteem. If others indicate their contempt or indifference to us, we feel vulnerable. But it is not just in our relationships with others that we can be made to feel inadequate. Our self-confidence is equally founded on ourselves and our own performance, particularly as measured against an ideal imposed from within ourselves as well as from the environment. Anyone exposed to frustration in attempting even a minor task is aware of how quickly our irritability level can rise. And how rapidly we can convert our dissatisfaction with ourselves into anger with some other. This conversion is a step that we all experience and is crucial to an understanding of the mechanism of scapegoating that will be presented later in the book.

My own personal frustration tolerance is at its lowest when performing fine hand movements, at which I am particularly untalented. Small parts in fine works are my particular nemesis–the tiny screw that must be positioned into the small opening under an extended ridge that is protected by a delicate filament or wire that must definitely not be disturbed. It is a situation that even in anticipation is sufficient to get my hands trembling with anticipated rage and frustration, and the trembling in turn is sure to disturb the wire that must remain inviolate for the mechanism to survive. Even in movies I find myself most anxious in those clichéd scenes where if a bomb is not defused, the good guys will be destroyed and the bad guys triumph. Such scenes inevitably produce in me a frisson of terror. It is the wise person who knows his own poisons and avoids them.

I am most tempted to enter my danger zones when dealing with electronic equipment, either in its assembly or repair. If what I am diddling with were an attempt to install or program a DVD player, the frustration that I experience has nothing at all to do with the typical image of frustration, that is, a frustrated *desire*. The desire to watch a movie is irrelevant. It is the evidence of my own personal ineptitude that threatens and, therefore, angers me.

What disturbs me is my knowledge that others can handle these matters quite well and that I seem to be particularly inept. The feeling of being all thumbs is not far from the feeling of having no hands. What enrages, because it frightens, is the emerging awareness of one's own inadequacy in relation to others–relative abilities, or lack thereof, in a competitive world.

Most of us are not frustrated by our inability to climb Mount Everest, accrue a fortune, or play golf like Tiger Woods. It is dealing with the computer glitches, fixing the plumbing, or roasting a turkey that triggers frustration. The apparent simplicity of these tasks suggests that others can do them easily. Philip Roth, in his marvelously honest book *Patrimony*, reveals his barely constrained rage at his irritable and demanding father, rage that breaks out when his father, in a tirade against his self-sacrificing girlfriend, complains that she cannot even pick out a decent melon. Roth's fury spills out, since he, like me, is obviously frustrated at his own inability to "pick out a decent melon," a task that others seem to manage. Our failure is more dramatic for being so relative. If I am incapable even here, where others succeed, what does that say about the worth and reliability of myself?

We can guard against a sense of impotence by deflecting the anger from the self to others, concentrating on who created the problem rather than who it is that cannot resolve it. If the example is audio equipment that a child tinkered with and damaged, one could divert the stream of anger from oneself to the child, withdrawing the attention from one's own inadequacy by finding a convenient, culpable target.

A more rational way to protect our self-esteem would be to avoid involvement in such trivia. Much of this is choice. Play football instead of golf. Don't play games at all. As for the handyman or household maintenance stuff of life that confounds us, we can admit defeat by hiring someone to do it. There is no disgrace in that. We live in a world of specialized work. We don't make our own clothes, grow our own vegetables, or hunt for our own meat. For most men "bringing home the bacon" is a metaphoric phrase that does not even involve their making a trip to the supermarket.

But what happens when we leave the world of the relatively trivial and avoidable? The learning-disabled child cannot avoid schooling, and at a time when we were all unsophisticated about such disabilities, she was expected to keep up. This is but a paradigm for that category of frustrations that may be imposed by unreasonable and unattainable standards. In a society where white—and only white—was beautiful, a black had few options except to attempt to transform himself into something approximating white, a hopeless, frustrating, and humiliating set of maneuvers.

Much has been made of the frustration of menial, unrewarding, unchallenging work that has no beginning or end, no product or pride, work that leads nowhere, with no hope of surcease. Still, there remains the honor, worth, and pride of fulfilling our responsibilities to ourselves and our dependents. When we are deprived of our capacity to work, that is a different order of things. The mass unemployment that exists in some areas of the underdeveloped world prevents people from finding the means of survival while at the same time denying them the sense of pride that work offers. When such frustration is imposed from outside, as occurs in the Palestinian refugee camps or the underdeveloped countries, the resulting diminution of self-pride and self-respect may be perceived as the product of an assault. Someone has invaded the repository of their dignity and robbed the people of the instruments of self-respect. But often it is the wrong someone who is blamed.

Frustration will always be most malignant when it involves those aspects central to the purposes of life. Because the frustrations we experience do not generally test us to our limits, most of us are not driven to the extreme of rage that leads to murder or suicide, the hatred that supports torture and inflicts suffering. In the privileged world we occupy, our frustrations are more likely to involve the luxuries and peripherals of life. When the areas that are frustrated are as central as work or sex, the anger that emerges is immense, evil, and ugly. Violent cases of frustrated rage are increasingly evident in the world today. I have not had personal experience with torturers or terrorists, but I have dealt extensively with similar hatred expressed in crimes of passion.

The passion in crimes of passion is the rage of frustrated potency, not of frustrated love, a common misrepresentation. Violent crimes of passion are for the most part acts not of a grieving lover but of a humiliated and impotent lover. In one typical case that I studied, a teenage boy stabbed to death a prepubescent girl in what was described as a sexual crime. It would have been better described as an asexual crime.

The young man was immature and sexually inhibited, having been raised in a religious but not abusive background. He was only fifteen and had never had any sexual experiences with girls, not uncommon in the small-town Canadian environment of that period. But he had, in addition, never been able to achieve an orgasm through masturbation. One Christmas season while working part-time in a department store, he lured an eight-year-old girl who had come to visit Santa Claus into the back stockroom where he worked.

He had the child undress and masturbated while looking at her nude body. At this point he had no desire to touch her and made no attempt to harm her. After twenty minutes of frustrating inability to reach an ejaculation, he became anxious and agitated. The frightened child began to whimper and cry. He then felt threatened by exposure and urgently told her to be still, which only further frightened her. In an attempt to silence her, in a combination of rage and terror, he picked up a knife that was at hand and stabbed her repeatedly and incessantly to death.

Humiliation

The added indignity that frenzied this adolescent boy was the humiliation of having exposed his impotence to the child, who, then, through her cries, threatened to further expose him to the community as a child molester. Every aspect of our behavior about which we are ashamed—the psychological conditions that confront us with a sense of our inadequacy and the danger that represents—are compounded when these deficiencies are made public. When the "fact" that we are less than lovable is exposed to the public eye, that we are less than potent is announced in the public space, that we are deprived and inadequate becomes part of the public knowledge, we experience humiliation of the most painful order.

Obviously this exposure invites potential exploitation by those who would take advantage of our weakness. But I do not believe that fear is the emotion that underlies humiliation. Shame is unquestionably the emotion present in this situation. We define ourselves, after all, not just as individuals, but as members of groups. We take pride not just in our accomplishments but in the recognition and acknowledgment of those accomplishments by the group in which we abide, in the appreciation of our worth by the community. To be reduced as an individual in our own eyes is bad enough. To be shamed before the group compounds our pain in a way that can readily convert anger into outrage, hurt into a humiliation, and that can ultimately pierce the boundaries of our constraint.

The rampage of an ex-employee at the workplace is often a product of such a perceived public humiliation, where the "public" may be only his fellow employees at the post office. Even here it is unlikely that this rage would lead to deadly and random shootings of innocent members of the community if it were not operating within the context of a paranoid ideation, the next stage of our consideration of hatred.

Just as an individual may be humiliated, so, too, may a population held in scorn rise to assert its indignation and restore its self-respect. There are such things as righteous indignation and righteous rage. These can lead to insurrection, revolution, and outright war.

I offer these categories of the dynamics of anger, not as a definitive list, but as a first step in understanding hatred, or at least the emotional underpinnings of hatred. As such, they are admittedly somewhat arbitrary and often overlapping. They do not pretend to be all-inclusive. They are only intended to indicate the multiple ways that individuals or groups can feel threatened. All threats lead to anger. All threats may be steps on the ladder to hatred.

Beyond direct threats are the equally frightening symbolic ones. They are proposed to explain how seeming "overreactions"—a response that seems inappropriate to the stimulus—can make sense when the metaphoric and symbolic nature of human existence is brought into consideration. These days we are rarely threatened by direct force, unless we are mugged or robbed. We are more likely to feel threatened by an assault on our reputation, our status, our livelihood, our manhood—or even a misperceived assault in these areas. We all live in the world of our own perceptions, where reality is only an occasional intruder.

Understanding the unconscious roots of rage, however, is only a first step in understanding hatred. Even when deprivation, injustice, betrayal, exploitation, frustration, or humiliation leads to violence, this ferocious rage is still not hatred. Rage can produce a slaughter of major proportions. There may even be transient pleasure in getting one's own back. But surely not sustained joy in witnessing the results of our unbridled rage. One would hope that in most cases, time would produce shame and contrition.

Rage, even murderous rage, is still short of hatred. Rage is anger at its most extreme. But it is only an emotion. In the throes of this powerful emotion, one may carry out a spontaneous action of the worst kind. Rage may lead to killing a perceived enemy in a frenzied moment, but not to dragging him alive behind a truck and watching his body being shredded and dismembered. Rage is a hot emotion; hatred is a cold passion. Rage explodes; hatred festers and may also then explode. Rage is only an emotion; hatred contains elements of the emotion of anger, including rage, but it is more. Hatred is an amalgam containing an emotion, a paranoid ideation, and an obsessive extended relationship to a perceived enemy.

5

ENVY

Locating an Enemy

M odern psychology has demonstrated the irrational nature of much of human behavior. We are not nearly as reasonable or logical as we would like to believe. When our emotions are in opposition to our rational judgments, we all too often succumb to the emotion. We will risk our life speeding on a highway—cut the bastard off, tailgate to intimidate—to defend some perverse sense of pride or honor or to retaliate for a sense of respect denied. Certainly when we are dealing with terrorism, torture, and hatred, we perceive clearly that something beyond reason is happening. Something "crazy" is going on.

Rage is the feeling that underlies all hatred. Frequently, rage is supported by a feeling of envy, another powerful and destabilizing emotion. Envy is not basic to all hatred, but is frequently a factor in defining the enemy on whom we will vent our spleen. Envy is particularly important in addressing the American perplexity as to why so much irrational hostility seems directed toward us.

I have always had difficulty in dealing with envy. In my attempts to understand the range of human emotions I have been guided by the doctrine of the "wisdom of the body"—and the mind. I believe that the broad range of human emotions is designed specifically to facilitate human beings in making rapid decisions—decisions essential in supporting individual or communal survival. The one emotion that seems to consistently resist this precept is the feeling of envy.

Envy may indeed be a useless emotion. It seems to serve none of the purposes of other emotions. Unlike the emergency emotions of fear and rage, it does not serve survival; unlike pride and joy, it does not serve aspiration, achievement, or the quality of our life; unlike guilt and shame, it does not serve conscience or community. It does not alert, liberate, or enrich us. It is ugly and demeaning. Unfortunately, it is still capable of motivating us. And it plays a crucial part in the mechanisms of hatred.

Envy has long fascinated moralists. It is represented in the Old Testament by the serpent in the Garden of Eden and is implicit in the covetousness that is prohibited in the tenth commandment. In the New Testament envy is described as the "evil eye," where—bracketed by wickedness, deceit, lasciviousness, and blasphemy—it takes its place among those "evil things that come from within, and defile the man."*

Poets and writers anticipated—albeit without the systematic approach—the works of modern psychologists and sociologists. There is nothing in Freud, our greatest psychologist, about the nature of human feeling and conduct that had not been portrayed by authors such as Euripides, Shakespeare, Molière, Balzac, Dickens, and Chekhov.

---

*Mark 7:22, 23 AV. All quotes from the New Testament are from the King James version. All quotes from the Hebrew Bible are from *Pentateuch and Haftorah*, ed. Dr. J. H. Hertz (London and New York: Soncino Press, 1987).

All the passion and pettiness of human existence are evident in the plays of Shakespeare. *Othello* is a textbook for the student who would contrast jealousy (Othello) and envy (Iago). Envy has occupied a prominent role in literature from the classic Greek drama into modern times. Milton defined envy as the devil's own emotion (as did Bacon). In *Paradise Lost*, Satan is filled with envy on viewing Adam and Eve in Paradise and in love and is determined to bring about their fall.* Grimm's German dictionary, compiled in the nineteenth century, in a brief definition of envy *(Neid)* included all of its elements, which later would be examined and expanded: "Envy expresses that vindictive and inwardly tormenting frame of mind, the displeasure with which one perceives the prosperity and the advantages of others, begrudges them these things and in addition wishes one were able to destroy or to possess them oneself: synonyms: malevolence, ill-will, the evil-eye."

I have defined envy as the bitter, resentful feeling that one has in the presence of and toward the person who is perceived as having traits superior to one's own. I used this crude and practical definition of envy in my practice, where many patients, in the anguish of their neuroses, were tormented by envy. Later, I would read Sir Francis Bacon's elegant and insightful essay on envy, in which he stated: "A man that hath no virtue in himself ever envieth virtue in others. For men's mind will either feed upon their own good or upon other's evil; and who wanteth the

---

*. . . aside the Devil turn'd
For envy, yet with jealous leer malign
Ey'd them askance, and to himself thus plain'd.
Sight hateful, sight tormenting! thus these two
Imparadis't in one another's arms
The happier *Eden*, shall enjoy their fill
Of bliss on bliss, while I to Hell am thrust.

one will prey upon the other; and whoso is out of hope to attain to another's virtue will seek to come at even hand by depressing another's fortune."*

Obviously, I am not using envy here in the vernacular sense, as a synonym for admire, as in "I envy you your patience (or drawing skills, musical abilities, way with women)." Such colloquial usages for feelings trivialize and minimize the malignancy of both the feelings and the individuals obsessed by them.

Envy is a complex amalgam of at least four conditions—all necessary for its full and true development. The first is that feeling of deprivation previously described. The mere absence of money, position, or pleasure will not alone generate a feeling of deprivation. We must go beyond the absence of goods. We must feel that this deprivation, far from being the common fate or even bad luck, was, to the contrary, imposed on us in particular. We must feel that someone has set out to deny us the good things of life. The feeling of deprivation requires imagining a malignant force in operation. Someone has done this to us.

Second, we must feel that what we have been denied is possessed by others. Crucial to envy is a comparative point of view. A sense of injustice and unfairness must prevail.

Third, we must have a sense of impotence in the face of the disparity. This impotence may exist because we are aware of our powerlessness to change our way of life or because there is no redress. Frustrated rage and helplessness are two essential ingredients in building envy. Over one hundred years ago, that great student of social unrest, Max Scheler,† emphasized the crucial role played by impotence. Scheler said that the mere fact that

---

*"Of Envy," *Francis Bacon: A Selection of His Works*, ed. Sidney Warhaft (New York: Macmillan, 1965), p. 64.

†Max Scheler, *Ressentiment* (New York: Schocken Books, 1972), pp. 48–50.

another possesses that which one covets does not constitute envy. It may, he suggests, motivate one to acquire the desired object or something similar by legal or illegal means, working for it, buying it, or stealing it. "Only when the attempt to obtain it by these means has failed, giving rise to the consciousness of impotence, does 'envy' arise."

The element that completes the mosaic of envy involves inserting a causal connection between our deprived state and the position of privilege of others. It is not just that we do not have that which they have, it is that we do not have it *because they* have it.

What possible adaptive value can such a demeaning emotion have? One might see it as a vestigial element from a prehistoric past. I have already indicated that I feel we are stuck operating with a physiology of anger that has been made obsolete by modern life. We resort to medical means to compensate for the adrenaline rush that has no place in a society where fight-or-flight solves few problems. Hence the large number of men and women taking beta-blockers and other drugs to stabilize their blood pressure and heart rates.

But of what value could envy have had in the prehistoric past? None that I can imagine, for it never brings gratification. We overvalue that which we do not have, and minimize that which we have been given. It is a game with no winning. The envious person would find misery in Eden.

Envy may simply be a degradation of the emotion of jealousy. Jealousy is admittedly a painful feeling, but its purposes can be traced to adaptational advantages. Jealousy is complicated by the fact that it has two separate meanings. In the sense that does not concern us here, jealousy refers to the suspicious, paranoid feeling associated with sexual and romantic attachments, where we are frightened that what we have might be stolen away. The jealousy that is relevant to this discussion is that form—often confused with envy—that focuses on what others have that we do not. Jealousy in early childhood is invariably involved with the rivalry for parental attention and affection. Jealousy emerges with the fear that the rival sibling is getting more than we are. In adult life, jealousy tends to be much less functional.

In precultural societies, jealousy may have served a similar role that it plays in childhood. It stirs competition. This promotes individual survival, while at the same time serving group survival in that it helps ensure that the fittest ascend to power. The fact that in our highly competitive and paranoid society, we need no spur to encourage competitive impulses does not belie the original useful purpose of the emotion.

In the case of envy, actual competition is not an essential. The envious person sees everything in a comparative and competitive framework, carrying envy into every aspect of life. Envy represents a vicious and hateful resentment of people that is independent of their actual encroachment on our pleasures. The envious resent everything about the other—their comfort, their possessions, and beyond that, their very existence.

Schadenfreude is the reverse of envy. Whereas envy generates pain in the pleasure of others—think of Satan's agony on viewing Adam and Eve in Paradise—schadenfreude is the joy felt on hearing of others' misery. All of us are likely to experience a certain pleasure when the high and the mighty take a fall. That simply reduces the gap between their power and ours. Schadenfreude, however, is a more severe problem. Envy and schadenfreude are obverses of the same coin, and always appear together. When severe, every success of even our closest friend will be viewed as a threat and a humiliation on our part. It is as though life is viewed as a seesaw where the rise of another human being demands our decline.

A young actress who had entered treatment with a mild depression was the first to present the most severe example of schadenfreude. One morning she arrived ecstatic and bubbling over with the news that she had just won a choice and featured part in a new play. It was the kind of part that garnered attention and could be a first step in a major career. And indeed it was.

I was a sophisticated therapist and knew enough about the tenacious quality of even mild depression—its resistance to actual achievement—to recognize that even though we had made significant progress in therapy, one event like this would not break the hold of the depression. Still, I was not prepared for the rage and despondency that emerged in her very next session. Morosely, she at first resisted all inquiries as to what had happened to dissipate the feeling of well-being that had been present only the day before. Finally, and reluctantly, she admitted with some chagrin that her change of mood was in response to a notice she had read in *Variety* that a close friend had been cast in a choice part in a movie.

When I questioned the vehemence of her response, her chilling answer was: "Don't you understand? In order for me to be happy, it is not enough that I succeed. My friends have to fail." Most of us can recall occasionally feeling some ambivalence—but not anguish—on hearing of a colleague's success or honor, even though that success was not at our own expense or in any way diminished our own opportunities. I have heard many similar responses from patients, an inordinately large number of them from actors. I assume that the intensity of competition in the field and the scarcity of adequate roles create something approaching a zero-sum game. In almost any other field, diligence, persistence, and talent will eventually bring success and recognition. That is simply not so in the world of the theater. Obviously, schadenfreude is not limited to any one group. I remember hearing from a prominent professional man—a generous man who had demonstrated minimal rancor during the course of his therapy—that in elections for honors or to honorary societies, he found himself routinely voting against those people he knew best.

Schadenfreude is a particularly revealing means of demonstrating the negative aspects of a free, but competitive, society. Obviously, we live in a competitive world; there are areas in which another's failure is in every way the equivalent of our success. Competitive sports is certainly such an area, and that may be one of its primary purposes, that is, to find a safe release for such competition. If my colleague bogies a hole, that is just as good as if I birdie the same one. In a running race, I win regardless of my speed or lack thereof if my opponent stumbles and falls. Similarly when I am running for office, my opponent's severe gaffe in a debate may be in every way the equivalent of my being particularly eloquent.

The spirit of competition will not explain the tendency to convert noncompetitive areas into competitions. It would not explain the competitive angst a lawyer might feel on hearing of the success of his scientist friend. Nor does it explain the envy experienced by a divorced woman over the happiness of her married friends. These are noncompetitive situations, but in the crabbed world of the envious, all prizes are perceived as stolen from them.

The readiness to interpret a chance event as an assault on self is emblematic of the tendency of the envious to see false causal relationship—the attribution of purpose or design where none exists. The psychological device of "projection," a key maneuver that links envy to paranoia, facilitates this tendency. Projection will be discussed in much more detail in subsequent chapters. Put simply, projection is the process by which we handle unworthy and unacceptable impulses arising from our own unconscious by attributing them to others.

A person who emerges from childhood with severe feelings of deprivation may carry with him into adulthood a desire to take from others that which he feels has been taken from him. Getting his own back. If this desire is actually perceived as legitimate, and if a perverse or absent conscience mechanism allows it, he may indulge this resentment in wanton acts of hatred. If, however, the feelings strike him as ignoble, he may project the feelings arising from within to others. The very feelings that he struggles with will then be perceived as arising from others and directed at him. This is the classic example of paranoid jealousy. It is almost a certainty that the jealous husband or wife is, at a minimum, obsessively preoccupied with illicit desires.

Jealousy is most often directed at what may be taken from us. Jealousy is anticipatory. It is fear of what is about to happen. Envy is driven by the past. There is a certainty that unfair deprivation has already occurred. With the envious person, anger and bitterness prevail because the injustice is perceived as already having happened. The emptiness and hunger are always present. "Consumed by envy" is an apt metaphor, and what is being consumed is pride and self-respect.

Chronic envy is an erosive, self-destroying disease. Like cancer, it eats away at the vitals of those who must live with it daily. When envy is a way of life, it converts the envious person into a grievance collector who masochistically embraces situations that confirm his deprivation and exploitation. If necessary, he himself will create such situations. He will interpret every ambiguous situation as a decision against him. Every route taken is the most heavily trafficked; his line at the checkout counters the slowest; his table at the restaurant the least desirable.

When the rage of frustration is joined by the irrational assumption that we are in a state of deprivation because "somebody" did this to us, we are on the road to hatred. Envy helps in locating an enemy when no more-convenient one is at hand. When the angry and envious person succeeds in locating another group on which he can fix responsibility for his deprivations, we have the essentials for prejudice and bigotry. But only when the other group or person becomes a fixation, an obsession, a passionate attachment, can a fixed hatred emerge. The distinction is crucial. Most racists in the American South did not participate in acts of violence against blacks. Not all antisemitic Germans joined in the revelries and mayhem of Krystalnacht. For such hateful acts, a social delusion is necessary, a thinking disorder must be present.

HATRED

AS A

THOUGHT DISORDER

6

UNDERSTANDING "NORMAL" BEHAVIOR

When an eighteen-year-old girl straps a fifteen-pound explosive pack—loaded with nails in order to maximize the extent and degree of slaughter—around her waist; enters a marketplace that is filled with other young women shopping for their evening meal; and proceeds to blow herself up for the singular purpose of crippling, maiming, blinding, and killing as many of her fellow creatures as possible, we are appalled. This is not how normal people behave. This is not consonant with the standards of human conduct as we understand them. We would assume the woman was psychotic—at least we would have assumed that in former times.

There have always existed among us those aberrant, unfortunate souls, those psychotic individuals, who have lost touch with reality and live in their own distorted world with its seemingly inexplicable sets of rules. Each thinks that he is the new Messiah, the Angel of Death, a special agent of the president of the United States, and each acts accordingly. We try to understand their illness and be forgiving of their actions. But we are not always successful, since their behavior is so alien to our sense of normal human conduct. Still, we draw a clear distinction between their behavior and the cultural standards of normalcy. Their random slaughter seems unmotivated, bizarre, and therefore monstrous.

What astonishes us with the Arab suicide bombers is that in their own community this behavior is perceived as rational. Beyond acceptance, it is actually glorified. Such conduct is elevated to a model to be embraced, admired, and emulated by their peers. Perhaps it is cynical to point out that many parents of the Palestinian suicide bombers have been paid $25,000 by Iraq and supplied a home and other comforts rare in these cultures of poverty. Children have been sold into slavery and prostitution in Africa, India, Pakistan, the Philippines, and other impoverished regions for a fraction of this amount. Still, the parents of the terrorists seem to take pride and joy in their children's behavior. Other parents aspire to the same fate for their children—or at least affect to.

And the religious leaders—the guardians and arbiters of morality in their community—join the political demagogues in celebration and endorsement of the murder and self-destruction. They do worse; they proclaim the bombers to be martyrs. It is positively dumbfounding to us that they idealize these monstrous acts, defining such behavior as being in the service of Allah—in the service of God, no less.

Is it possible to view terrorism as simply a function of cultural variability? Given the disparate potentials of human behavior, should we acknowledge terrorism as an authentic example of cultural diversity? Can we acknowledge it as normal behavior? Or are we entitled to label such action as a perversion of human nature?

The diversity of human behavior *is* astonishing. Each human infant is born incomplete, awaiting the variable impacts of family

and culture to determine what emerges. Environmental influences modify the genetic structures and thus the very form and
nature of human life in ways impossible with any other animal.
And the line between normal and sick behavior is as porous a
boundary as the border between Afghanistan and Pakistan.
Defining sick behavior is contingent on defining the normal, and
that is not so easy, given the singularity of the human species, the
range of normal lifestyles available to our species, and the diversity of our behavior and our cultures. We must understand the
boundaries of normalcy.

The arguments about normal and perverse—hatred and evil—
are but part of an ongoing dialogue about human nature itself.
Two contrasting views prevail. One is expressed most clearly in
the beginning of the Old Testament: "So God created man in His
own image, in the image of God created He him; male and fe-
male created He them."* This statement definitively places man
apart from the continuity of the beasts. Being in the image of a
righteous and just Lord, man must by nature be endowed with
goodness. And as the Bible later confirms: "Thou hast made him
but little lower than the angels, and hast crowned him with glory
and honor."† The Bible, in allowing our species the freedom to
rebel, gave rise to the Christian doctrine of original sin. Whereas
the Old Testament emphasizes an inborn goodness that is cor-
ruptible, the New Testament emphasizes an inborn corruptness
that is correctable.

The view from the second half of the twentieth century—conditioned by two world wars, the Holocaust, the atom bomb, and
growing ecological disasters—lent credence to an opposing view of
human nature supporting those who viewed human nature as

---

*Genesis 1:27.

†Psalm 8:4–5.

inherently selfish and evil. The world of modern anthropologists and ethologists tended to support a gloomy view of man as the destroyer.* These sociologists may be seen as the descendants of Montaigne, the most extreme spokesman for the vileness of natural man. Montaigne viewed man as not just an animal, but a lesser animal. The very traits that are generally proposed as our glories—our freedom and autonomy—were perceived by him as primarily the freedom to do evil. As such freedom is a baser phenomenon than the instinctually driven behavior of lower animals.†

The negative view of nature has been buttressed by the powerful emotional impact of evil since 9/11. This view is also supported by our tendency to be more fascinated by evil than virtue, discomfort than comfort, sickness than health. Look at the evening news. One manifestation of the view that we are innately evil, needing civilization to live in harmony, is expressed by the following: When a human being behaves like an animal, he is often described as having "lost control," as though it is only conscious control that reins in our bestiality; we are presumed to be rampant individuals pursuing our own survival at any cost. However, when a parent sacrifices herself for a child, it is never described as a "loss of control."

Obviously, no one can deny the ample evidence of morally bad behavior. But neither ought one deny the evidence of the opposite. There are noble acts of selflessness, generosity, empathy, sharing, caring, and even self-sacrifice. The difference is in

---

*See the writings of Konrad Lorenz, Robert Ardrey, Lionel Tiger, Robin Fox, and Desmond Morris.

†See "Apology for Raymond Cibonne," in *Essays of Montaigne* (New York: Modern Library, 1946). The arguments about the cost of freedom, as well as the fact of freedom, have been universally addressed. For an insightful and elegant take on this theme see "The Grand Inquisitor" in Dostoyevsky's great novel *The Brothers Karamazov.*

that which "comes naturally." One group chooses to see human beings as survival-oriented hedonists whose aggressiveness is contained only by the restricting forces of civilization. This group views unselfishness as an attribute that must be indoctrinated into the actions of the individual by a controlling culture. The other group sees caring as innate, but capable of being destroyed by a lack of proper nurture.

Freud straddled both camps but ended up on the side of a norm for decency. He was aware of the bizarre extended helplessness of the human child and the biological mandate for adult care and sympathy. Since the fate of the species could not depend on some learned control patterns on the part of parents, he had to assume that care for the helpless child must be guaranteed by nature, not simply learned. Caring is not like chemistry or piano playing, something that must be taught. Caring must be part of the genetic mandate of our species. A tender and protective attitude to the newborn—and by extension to the innocent and the helpless—is innate.

If we accept this premise, one can not suspend moral judgment of certain behavior by attributing it to cultural diversity. There are at least some norms and values that cross political and cultural boundaries. There are some absolute criteria of good and evil. Encouraging innocent children to destroy other innocent children for political purposes is evil. How can we cope with such evil? Only by confronting and understanding it. Only by seeing the links that tie pathological to normal behavior. Therefore we need to examine the decidedly strange conduct of "normal" people before analyzing the pathological aspects of behavior.

We do not conduct our lives like the ants, in a predictable pattern designed to support our survival. We are capable of being unpredictable to the point of self-destructiveness. The fact that we are animals endowed with rationality unfortunately does not mean that we are rational animals. The possession of reason does not ensure reasonableness. At least not all the time. One has only to look at the crazy pace and pursuits of life in our times to know that something besides survival is at stake and that something other than reason is driving us to our goals. Think of the tobacco industry, where executives spend their lives encouraging people to kill themselves by utilizing their products. And think of the people who buy these products in the face of the clearest evidence that lung cancer is an elected option, the one malignant disease we are all free to escape.

Many of us, bankers and brokers, hucksters and peddlers, devote seventy to eighty hours each week to grinding and unrewarding work, waiting for the opportunity to retire. Is there anything that money can buy that is worth the time spent earning it in often deadening and sometimes immoral pursuits—in dissipation of energy and self-respect? And here we are talking about presumably normal behavior, as distinguished from the pathological actions of terrorists.

Human conduct is obviously not analogous to the practice of engineering. We do not take the best available evidence and apply it to the problem at hand. We do not design our lives the way we design bridges. But before we can deal with something so irrational as paranoia and psychopathic conduct, we must deal with the "irrational" elements of normal people in their everyday life—if only to be able to draw a moral distinction between them and the crazy and aberrant.

Normal human beings operate in what had for years seemed mysterious ways, best explained elliptically through the creative insights of our great writers. With the birth of modern psychology in the latter half of the nineteenth century, the study of normal behavior—perception, memory, learning, and motivation—was put on scientific footing. This was quickly followed by a systematic attempt to understand pathological behavior. Out of that crush of insight and genius emerged one towering figure who attempted to fuse the two, Sigmund Freud.

Oh, how this mighty figure who dominated intellectual life in the first half of the twentieth century has fallen in recent decades! The oversell and overkill of psychoanalytic theory promised an explanation for all behavior and relief from all mental illness. No theory could ever fulfill the expectations of all this hype. But the disillusionment with what it failed to achieve—a cure for mental illness—must not obscure what it did accomplish; it supplied us with one of the most comprehensive and usable theories of normal human motivation. Certain Freudian insights can help us in understanding the variety of normal experience and also the limits of normalcy. By establishing the boundaries of even so irrational an animal as the human being, we will be able to understand the neurotic and psychotic extensions that lead to hatred and terror.

The contributions of Freud that have stood the test of time—and have been absorbed into commonsense understanding of how we behave—can be grouped into the following:

1. We are not all as rational as we like to think. Freud assaulted the cockiness and arrogance of the technological optimists at the birth of the twentieth century by pointing out the limits of reason. He focused on the emotions that are often the hidden drivers of our actions, the sexual instinct and our aggressive needs. Admittedly he overemphasized the role of the sexual drive, but in the process he forced us to attend to the passions. He insisted that the rationale we offer for our behavior is often only "rationalization" (a word to which he gave its modern meaning) after the fact, disguising the emotionally driven intent of the behavior.

2. We are not as free as we like to think. Many present-day actions are a product of our treatment in the past. This explains why seemingly like individuals will behave differently in the face of the same crisis. It explains why one person, when faced with

an assailant, will run with fear, another attempt to appease or ne-gotiate, and a third recklessly attack. This is a developmental point of view. When one says that we do "this" because of how we were treated by our parents in the past, there is the sugges-tion that "this" is not that freely selected an action. Such dy-namic explanations have been labeled psychic determinism and have been viewed by many as a direct assault on free will. Most psychoanalysts "believe" in free will, but they are forced to strug-gle with a theory that drives one to conceding profound limits to human autonomy.

3. We are not as insightful or self-knowing as we pretend. Nothing we do is caused by a simple stimulus-response mecha-nism. We do not make a decision at the moment, even though we may perceive it as happening that way. All behavior is a complex result of a number of forces and counterforces operating on us at that moment. Some of these influences arise from the past, some emerge out of the immediate present; some of our motives are operating consciously, others unconsciously and without our knowledge. All of these forces and counterforces act in concert, and their balance determines the specific action: Do we stop to help the elderly woman who fell in the street or do we walk on? Will we go on a diet or simply rationalize about it? Will we un-comfortably tell the truth or will we tell the convenient white lie? Will we act courageously or cowardly in the face of a crisis? This balancing of forces and counterforces driving us one way or the other constitutes a dynamic view of behavior—hence the term "psychodynamics." This conception also threatens the view of our own autonomy and rationality to which we cling so dearly.

4. We are less individual than we like to think. Actually, we are obligate social animals; we live in groups because we must. Other people are as essential to our survival as food, water, and oxygen. Therefore, exclusion from the group is a terrifying concept. The threat of ostracism becomes a potent means for forcing individu-

als to conform their behavior to the dictates of the community or its leaders.

5. We live in a world of our own perception, to which actuality, that is, the real world, takes a secondary role. Once we go beyond the struggle for food and shelter, the basic struggle for survival, we enter into the world of our own imagination. Pride and shame, joy and despair, security or terror, will be fixed by our *perception* of what is happening, which only accidentally in rare moments will correspond with what is *actually* going on. This locates Freud in the tradition of German philosophical idealism, which dominated his education and milieu.

The emphasis on the perceived world as the arena for human operations was not an original construct of Freud's. It can be traced back to classic times. Epictetus, a Stoic philosopher, is quoted as saying: "What disturbs and alarms man are not the things, but his opinions and fancies about the things." What Freud did was take ideas that were common currency in the philosophical world of the academy and apply them to the scientific study of human behavior then emerging from the psychological laboratories and the psychiatric clinics of Europe. But who could have predicted what followed from that? Freudian psychology, flowing out of its original clinical environs, saturated the entire intellectual community and, in the process, transformed our very view of ourselves.

There was no area of creative activity that was untouched by Freudian influence, from surrealist paintings to plays, biography, literary criticism, and poetry. Nothing was immune, not movies, not haute couture. Dream sequences became de rigeur even in Broadway musicals, the former venue of double takes, pratfalls, showgirls, and chorus lines.

People began to think and talk about their lives in terms of their unconscious desires, hidden motives, projections, idealizations, rationalizations, sublimations, repressions, self-delusions, and ego trips. And these were the most grounded and least fanciful concepts. Then there were the exotics: penis envy, castration anxiety, Oedipal and Electra complexes, Eros and Thanatos.

The Freudian insights launched a democratic assault on the ramparts of Victorian society: its morality, its scientific optimism, its class distinctions, its rationalism. Freud leveled old distinctions and upset the traditional standards for human conduct established during the Victorian age. He introduced a wild card into the deck. He proclaimed everything as either directly or indirectly sexual, which of course was idiotic, but in the process it legitimated libidinal drives and started the sexual revolution, which would continue through the twentieth century. Freudian theory openly proclaimed that sexual appetite was ubiquitous, universal, and respectable. Everyone did it or thought about doing it. This proved liberating. Sex was no longer vulgar but the repository of the life force. We all acted under the influence of our libidos: aristocrat and commoner, man and woman, the elderly and the infant. Perversity was not just for the perverted. We all carried such impulses deep within our ids. Freud ushered in an electrifying and creative era.

What was not so sanguine, however, was the unintended effect of what became known as the Freudian revolution on the basic principle of responsibility. The revolution made a tragic and profound contribution to the moral relativism that has fudged the concept of evil, leading to a substitution of understanding for justice.

Without a clear sense of responsibility, there is no morality. Without the same sense of responsibility, the law cannot function. Psychic determinism shredded to tatters our sense of human autonomy. Courts of law became courts of nonculpability, with itinerant psychologists acting as court jesters.

On December 7, 1993, Colin Ferguson boarded the 5:33 P.M. commuter train to Hicksville, Long Island, pumped thirty rounds of ammunition and sprayed his fellow commuters, managing to kill six people and wound nineteen others. The mayhem was limited only because a heroic passenger overcame him before he could reload. The ever-imaginative defense lawyer, Ron Kuby, a colleague of William Kunstler, decided that his plea of not guilty could be supported by the fact that Ferguson was suffering from "black rage." What is black rage? Well you might ask. It turns out that it is some "malignant psychological state" black people endure by dint of being raised in a white racist society.

What a blessing that most black Americans living in the United States have not developed this maddening psychological condition that drives one to mass murder. At the risk of being a spoilsport, let me mention that Colin Ferguson was raised as an affluent member of the decidedly black culture of Jamaica. There he suffered the indignities of being chauffeured back and forth in an expensive limousine from his expensive home to his expensive private school.

Even Colin Ferguson seemed offended by this defense. He refused to use the plea, firing his lawyers instead. Still, the "black rage" defense lives on. It has been used in many courtrooms to explain and thus exculpate not only gratuitous black violence against whites but also black crimes against Hispanics, Indians, Koreans, and assorted other minority groups.

Not to be outdone, defense attorney Erik M. Sears introduced the equally compelling diagnostic category, "early Arab trauma," in defense of his client, Rashid Baz. In March 1994, Baz had opened fire with an automatic weapon on a group of children on their way to a yeshiva. This was no impulsive maneuver. Baz planted himself on the Brooklyn Bridge, carefully timing the arrival of the bus. Because he was shooting at a moving target, he was able to kill only one student, sixteen-year-old Aaron Halberstam, but he managed to seriously wound three others.

Attorney Sears—lacking any serious defense for this premeditated slaughter of the innocents—emulated Kunstler and Kuby and proclaimed his client the victim. Baz had spent the first eighteen years of his life in Lebanon. He could not possibly be held responsible for this murder. He had been so psychologically scarred by the larger environment of his youth that he had no more understanding or control over his behavior "than a fire once lit understands why it's burning." All that was necessary was to locate an expert witness to lend scientific credibility to the defense. He had no trouble locating Nuha Abuddabeh, a Ph.D. in psychology, a practicing clinician, and the hostess of her own talk show, no less. It was she who introduced the disease "early Arab trauma" into the lexicon of psychologically exculpating conditions.

Logically, this disease would seem to exculpate all people who were raised in an Arab culture for the first eighteen years of their lives from criminal charges of murder. If so, it could equally be grounds for banning this population—psychically incapable of controlling their murderous rage—from entering the country. While denigrating these defenses as ludicrous, I acknowledge both Ferguson and Baz to be "sick" people. But common people using common sense will almost inevitably convict them in a courtroom. And they should.

All "mental illness" cannot be a free ticket to exoneration. "To understand all is to forgive all" is not an operative principle except in the psychiatrist's office—in the context of medicine— where the patient is granted certain special privileges and understanding. Inherent in the definition of the "sick role" is the principle of nonculpability. The sick person is a victim, not a criminal. He is not to be held responsible and punished for his illness, whether that illness is typhoid fever, which can infect others and kill them, or schizophrenia, which can also produce behavior that kills others. That is all true in the sick room. But not in the courtroom and, for that matter, not in the mind of the ordinary person.

Unfortunately, at the same time that psychiatrists were continuing to defend the nonculpability inherent in the sick role, psychiatry was vastly expanding the definition of mental illness. The population of those with some symptoms of mental illness came to include the majority. Still, the courts, in order to secure a society of law, had to defend the idea of a populace acting voluntarily and freely, therefore responsible for their actions. How could the courts do that, when almost everybody was now assumed to be a little sick?

When confronted with this dangerous contradiction in definition and purpose, two distinguished students of human behavior articulated two opposing, and equally unmanageable, solutions. One decided that there was no such thing as mental illness. And the other announced that there was no such thing as human freedom.

In 1961 Thomas Szasz published his immensely influential book, *The Myth of Mental Illness*, and became a hero of both the libertarian Right and the libertarian Left, who shared his antiauthoritarian and antiestablishment sentiments. In this book, as the title suggests, Szasz denied the very existence of a population of the mentally ill.

The 1960s was a period that chose to romanticize the insane as saner than the rest of us, as demonstrated in such movies as *The King of Hearts* and *One Flew over the Cuckoo's Nest*. It took a long time for the liberal supporters of Szasz to realize that if you deny the validity of mental illness, the only proper place for a schizophrenic man dangerous to others was a prison—as Szasz, himself, would state.

At the other extreme was the brilliant psychologist B. F. Skinner. In his influential book *Beyond Freedom and Dignity*, published in 1971, Skinner denied the very existence of freedom, thus any voluntary action. In his image of human behavior, the adult is tied to his past by connecting bonds of conditioned responses that force him into predictable and patterned responses. Skinner thus links Homo sapiens to the lowest living creatures in one seamless continuum. Autonomy is a myth that human beings perpetuate about themselves to narcissistically assert their superiority to lower animals.

Nevertheless, most of us are prepared to accept both: a concept of human freedom, with its element of accountability for action; and a category of the mentally ill, who being sick must not be held fully responsible for their behavior. Simple prudence must be exercised. Both constructs, autonomy and mental illness, need a little pruning at the edges. And if we approach the problem with a clear head, we can allow these contradictory theories of human behavior to coexist. In certain contexts we must assume one, while in other contexts we are obliged to accept the alternative.

Obviously, Colin Ferguson and Rashid Baz are not normal variants of their cultures. They are individuals obsessed with hatred. Their behavior is clearly pathological. They would undeniably be diagnosed as mentally ill by a modern psychiatrist—as would be the murderers of Matthew Shepard, the Oklahoma City bombers, and the men who chained James Byrd, Jr., to the back of a truck, dragging him to his death. All of them would be sent to jail by a jury of their peers. And rightly so. There is sick and then there is "sick."

7

UNDERSTANDING "SICK" BEHAVIOR

The average physician starts the diagnostic process by taking a history, a testament to the continuing importance of symptoms even in this day of CAT scans and MRIs. A doctor wants to hear the patient's "complaints." Is he suffering from headache, tightness in the chest, excessive thirst, or undue fatigue? Is he demonstrating shortness of breath, dizziness, insomnia? The doctor is directed to further investigations by the nature of these symptoms.

The psychiatrist approaches her patient in the same way. She is interested in emotional and mental symptoms. These can be particularly confusing, especially in modern times where the definition of mental illness has been expanded well beyond its original conception and the terminology has become more complicated. "Abnormal," "sick," "crazy," and "insane" are confusing terms, used quite differently in different environments and by different observers. At times the same observer adopts different attitudes toward the same behavior, dependent on the context. As a psychiatrist, I am prepared to accept rude and aggressive behavior from my patients in my office that I would not tolerate from others. Such behavior in the framework of a therapeutic relationship would not even be labeled "rude." It would be analyzed for its unconscious motives. I am not interested in the "unconscious motives" of the ugly drunk at the bar—nor for that matter, of a friend in my living room—and am not prepared to passively and benignly endure such behavior.

The hatred that is of concern here is by my definition a psychological phenomenon. An essential premise of this book is that hatred is rarely a rational response to a real threat or affront. Acts of hatred represent displacements of an internal conflict onto external sources. They are "symptoms" of a basic emotional disorder. Hatred is obsessive, irrational, self-serving, and ultimately—like any other symptom—self-destructive. We, however, do not grant an act of hatred the same immunity from judgment or punishment that we would when a psychological phenomenon is perceived as a symptom of a disease. We use a different set of criteria in the public political arena. The therapeutic attitude should have little influence there.

The problem of judgment, culpability, and punishment is complicated by the fact that the constituency of terrorists comprises at least three distinct populations. The single, lone-wolf terrorist—what I call the entrepreneurial terrorist—is often a confused and psychotic loner. The institutional terrorists, those who join Al Qaeda, Hamas, and other terror groups, may act in a manner that seems equally insane. but they are not psychotic; they know exactly what they are doing. The members of the professional SS *Einsatzgruppen*, who volunteered to slaughter the Jews by hand before the Nazis built their gas furnaces, were largely psychopaths or, at the very least, individuals with severe character disorders.* For purposes of justice as well as our own self-defense, we must handle these groups quite differently. But first, we must attend to the often confusing terminology used to distinguish among them.

Abnormal Behavior

Normal behavior refers to conformity, conforming to "a norm, standard, pattern, level or type." So what is abnormal behavior for a human being? The question can be answered only by a series of other questions. Am I referring to physiological behavior? Interpersonal behavior? Public or private? In relation to the standards of the species or of the culture? If the latter, what are the cultural norms and can they be considered normal?

The problem of defining behavior relates to the uniqueness of that perverse species, Homo sapiens. It is easier with lower animals. Consider the single-celled animals. Observing these simplest of creatures under a microscope, one is impressed by both their anatomical similarities, one to another—they are all essentially formless blobs—and by the identical quality of their behavior. The amoeba randomly bounces from one place to another, absorbing nutrients and excreting wastes. That's about it. And it does not matter if the swamp water in which it lives is in Toronto or Timbuktu.

In the case of the amoeba, normal behavior is easy to describe, since there can be little variation from the norm. The simplicity of the amoeba's functions allows for nothing abnormal short of cellular destruction. These single-celled creatures are the purest

---

*See Richard Rhodes's brilliant book, *Masters of Death: The SS-Einsatzgruppen and the Invention of the Holocaust* (New York: Knopf, 2002).

individualists—they do not even require another individual to re-produce; they simply split themselves asunder, creating two where there was one. Still, it is hard to treat them as individuals. It is safe to assume no protozoologist names or romanticizes these simple creatures. They have no individuality. In contrast, I have a dear herpetologist colleague with whom I have collabo-rated in research on "animal rights" who ascribes emotions and personality to his cold and slithery charges, upbraiding me for being a "speciesist" with a bias toward warm-blooded animals.

We do not have to examine each step of the taxonomic ladder from species to genus to family of man to appreciate the increas-ing complexity of the animals. However, their increased biologi-cal complexity is not accompanied by a proportional increase or variability of lifestyle. Obviously, a primatologist distinguishes among the members of her gorilla or chimpanzee horde. They look and behave differently even to the eyes of amateur ob-servers at a zoo. But one horde of apes does essentially that which all hordes do. In that sense, their conformity to type is only somewhat more varied than such lower mammals as hyenas or lions, or even the amoebas. This conformity makes it easier for the biologist to spot the abnormal members of his group.

When a raccoon ambles up to a larger predator like a human being in broad daylight, we know that its behavior is abnormal. It is not supposed to be active in the daytime hours, and it is reck-lessly approaching an animal that can and does hunt it. Life-endangering behavior is anomalous to most species. It is acting abnormally, and probably *is* sick in the physical sense of that word. This behavior is the sign of a rabid raccoon. When despite all the posted warnings, a human being approaches a dangerous bear in Yellowstone Park, we do not presume he is sick. We think of him as stupid. And to judge from the number of visitors killed or maimed by bears in the parks, his behavior is not that singular or unconventional.

It is the discontinuity of the human species from the rest of the animal kingdom, discussed in the previous chapter, that makes a judgment of sickness more problematic. More of our behavior is free of instinctual fixation. We are free to look differently, dress differently, live differently, in different climates and different terrain, and to behave differently in our daily activities. Since we spend relatively little time hunting for food these days—an activity that dominates the life of most animals—we are free to work rather than just labor to survive, and the work at which we spend the majority of our waking hours varies dramatically. We become accountants and acrobats, farmers and plastic surgeons, spending the majority of our time in wildly different pursuits.

For these reasons, we have been generous in setting the borders of normalcy for human behavior, allowing serious deviations from a standard before necessarily labeling the behavior as abnormal. In terms of emotional behavior, we accept the extrovert and the recluse as within accepted standards. All manner of nonconforming behavior is sanctioned. Even with something as primary to species survival as the sexual drive, we allow great latitude, sexually permissive communities coexisting with celibate ones. Nevertheless, since the beginning of recorded time, certain people and certain behavior have stood out. They are the outsiders, beyond the perimeters of the defined normal.

Sick Behavior

Early literature is filled with the strange and the exotic persons who even in those days were described as mad—people who were identified by their peers as having significantly departed from the wide landscape of normal human behavior. The madness was extreme and complete: like the madness of King Saul, poignant and terrible to behold; the frightful vengeance of Medea; Nebuchadnezzar, who "did eat grass as oxen, and his body was wet with the dew of heaven, till his hairs were grown like eagles' feathers and his nails like birds' claws."* Nebuchadnezzar's appearance is an apt description of that of a deteriorated and neglected schizophrenic living on the streets of our major cities.

The assignment of the cause of such extreme behavior differs from culture to culture. Deranged people were considered cursed, enchanted, possessed by demons, or holy visionaries. In the case of Nebuchadnezzar, his behavior was perceived as a punishment from God, to whom he had dared compare himself. In some cases the behavior was seen as a gift and the eccentric viewed as a prophet. With the emollient influence of time we view Saint Francis dressed in rags and speaking to the animals differently from the way we perceive the homeless man dressed similarly and having his words with who knows whom. Until the eighteenth century, symptoms that today would be generally reserved for the insane were interpreted as special gift, a sign of the holy. Or they might equally be viewed as a sign of bewitchment, and the person would be destroyed as a henchman of evil, a witch or a warlock. The pathetic teenagers exploited by their mullahs to destroy themselves while destroying others will draw different evaluations from the Arab and the Israeli populations. And history will judge them differently, too.

These days we are unlikely to designate a deranged person as a saint or demon. Instead we designate the irrationality that defies normal human understanding as crazy. Crazy behavior is often animal-like and wantonly destructive (running amok), or simply a feckless and dangerous insensibility to self-interest. One sign that has been central to an assessment of mental illness in any individual is his wanton lack of interest in even the basic need for food and shelter, the cardinal essentials for survival.

---

*Daniel 4:32 AV.

Almost from the beginning of modern society, a concept of insanity was a clearly entrenched standard in most countries. The Bethlem Royal Hospital in England—Bedlam—was commissioned specifically for the care and confinement of the mentally ill sometime around the year 1400. And the appreciation that the insane ought not be held responsible for their actions goes back centuries. Nigel Walker, in his classic work, *Crime and Insanity in England,** cited the first case of a man actually freed by a jury for reasons of insanity, dating it back to 1505 (in tragic parallel to our times, the crime was infanticide). In all such cases, a clear line was drawn between "them" and "us." Their behavior was grotesque and their actions beyond human understanding.

Coexisting with this humane and modern view of the insane was the concept of "possession" by dybbuks, devils, and demons. This was most dramatically evidenced by the infamous Salem witch trials of 1692. A parallel confusion exists in our minds today. Even in these days of enlightenment, when someone says to us, "You're sick," or says in relation to an action of ours, "That's sick," it is rarely stated in sympathy of our condition—an acknowledgment of our asthma or our cancer. It is certainly not an expression of support and compassion. It is the exact opposite of the traditional attitude toward sickness, which includes blamelessness for symptoms. It represents a severe moral condemnation, another way of saying "that's disgusting and abhorrent." This attitude is but one sign of a persistent ambivalence toward mental illness.

No real attempt at a *scientific* understanding of sickness, physical or mental, would emerge until the latter half of the nineteenth century. With a stunning burst of creativity, modern medicine was born in the research laboratories of Europe by

---

*Nigel Walker, *Crime and Insanity in England* (Edinburgh: Edinburgh University Press, 1968).

such distinguished scientists as Pasteur, Koch, Ehrlich, Semmel-weis, Wundt, Helmholtz, and Virchow. We began to understand the nature of physical illness and were on our way to discovering the cures.

Still, there was no concept of anything called mental disease, that is, disease of the mind, as distinguished from disease of the brain. Insanity was conceptualized in the same way as one viewed heart disease: as being a product of organ damage or system deterioration. And at that time this view was adequate. Most of the mental conditions that were recognized in the nineteenth century were actually the result of brain damage, a product of stroke, degenerative senile changes, or the damage wrought on the brain by late-stage syphilis, the leading cause of admission to insane asylums. It was easy then to view mental illness as brain disease. If liver functions failed, the liver was damaged. If thinking was disordered, there must be brain damage.

The body itself was envisioned in the same terms as other physical structures, a collapsing roof or a leaky cistern. Sickness was the product of wear and tear of age, a traumatic injury, or an invasive organism, such as the newly discovered bacteria. Since behavior was perceived as a product of the brain and peripheral nervous system, mental illnesses were called "nervous disorders," and the physician looked for physical malfunctions in the nervous system to repair. In those early days, the behavioral abnormalities that concerned medicine and the courts were those at the extreme periphery of human conduct, those that would be described by laymen as crazy, lunatic, or insane. They were what we today would call the major psychoses. All that would change with the revolutionary work of Sigmund Freud at the beginning of the twentieth century.

Freud, a neurologist, was attracted to a series of conditions called "the hysterias." Hysteria is not to be confused with the current usage of the word "hysteria" as in "acting hysterical," that is, being overemotional. Hysteria, as it was understood in the nineteenth century, was an illness characterized by a physical symptom that had no demonstrable physical damage to the affected organ: for example, blindness with no damage to the structure of the eye or the optic nerve. Or more curiously, a symptom that could not possibly be explained anatomically. Such a condition was glove anesthesia; a patient would exhibit a hand numb from the wrist down. This is an actual impossibility, since the sensory nerves run in a linear track from the armpit to the finger, not in annular circles around the hand. Nerve damage would cause anesthesia in a line down the arm and into the thumb, let's say, sparing the other fingers.

After years of investigation, Freud came to the startling conclusion that these "neuroses," as they were called—literally nervous inflammations—had nothing to do with the status of nerve fibers but were products of psychological conflicts and the stress that they produced. This conclusion was a monumental departure from the prevailing medical model of disease formation. Freud dared to suggest that feelings and ideas as well as poisons, trauma, or invading organisms could cause disease. His audacious statement that "the hysteric suffers from reminiscences" infuriated a medical community that had finally achieved scientific legitimacy by locating the physical causes of disease in damaged organs. Freud was now saying that for certain diseases the causes were not physical and the organs remained undamaged. He paid in ridicule and censure.

Freud honored mental illness by applying to it the same rigorous standards of study that were then being applied to the burgeoning understanding of physical disease. He not only discovered the tools for understanding the human condition, but he applied those tools to the newly created field of mental illness. He created the equivalent of a physiology of mental illness. By that I mean that he carefully tracked the normal internal mental processes—the physiology of the mind, and looked for the distortions, the pathology, that lead to mental illness.

In the days before the discovery of the germ theory, diseases were labeled according to their symptoms. Patients suffered from fevers, agues, and chills. What was then described as the illness was often the visible manifestation of the body's *defense* against the illness—the symptoms. A fever is an elevation of body temperature designed to enhance the chemical reactions brought into play to fight the offending organism—not yet identified. As any cook knows, heating increases the rate of chemical responses. The body "knows" this automatically.

The inflamed and ugly boil marks the entrance of a toxin, foreign body, or bacterial agent disturbing the integrity of a bodily tissue or function. The body responds to the attack with an immune response. It rushes white cells to the spot, increases the vascularity in the area to facilitate the delivery of blood elements that fight the invader, and ratchets up the heat to speed the chemical responses. A boil, when examined, is therefore red, hot, inflamed, and filled with pus. None of these is the "disease"—a staphylococcus infection—but a sign of the body's defensive maneuvers against the invading microbe. The boil is a perfect "compromise formation" having elements of both cause and defense against the physical trauma. Freud suggested very similar mechanisms for psychic trauma.

In a somewhat grandiose attempt to find a universal theory—like Marx and Einstein—Freud evolved the Libido theory. This theory postulated the rather absurd idea that all behavior could be understood as an expression of the sexual drive and its vicissitudes. Unfortunately, Freud's followers, the "Freudians," tenaciously held onto these early concepts as though they were religious testaments. Eventually, this loyalty led to the increasing disillusionment with psychoanalysis as a treatment form and the demise of Freud's reputation in current times.

Nevertheless, those psychoanalysts like me who abandoned the Libido theory continued to use the most basic Freudian principles of human motivation to analyze aberrant social behavior. We would accept the idea of internal conflict, but cast that conflict in terms of different and varied sources of psychic distress. Once liberated from the need to always see a sexual underpinning to psychological tensions, we found that conflict could be located in all sorts of internal desires. Psychic stress could be generated in all the various areas of aspiration and failure that occupy the human being in his daily life. A person could be conflicted by power, aggression, authority, anger, guilt, humiliation, or pride.

Internal conflict often arises from dependency. An analysis of the manipulated populations in Africa and the Arab world indicates that their emasculating dependency, not their poverty, drives them to genocidal hatred. Dependency forces us to inhibit and constrain our desires when they bring us into conflict with those on whom we are dependent. Someone enraged at a despotic authority figure is frustrated by his inability to express that hatred, particularly when that figure is a parent, an employer, a religious leader, or a despotic tyrant and his lackeys. Our rage and our fear of the consequences of releasing this rage create the kind of conflict that underlies much neurosis. For such rage to be released safely, it must be displaced to a neutral person or group in the environment with whom one can be angry without fear of the consequences. A scapegoat must be found.

Symptoms, such as the glove anesthesia of hysteria, are devices that facilitate living with conflict or avoiding despair. Failures and guilt can be—in the terms of psychoanalysis—"rationalized," "projected" to others, "denied," or converted into successes by "delusion formation." All these strategies serve to make the unbearable present bearable by mitigating our own impotence in the face of the dilemma and our own responsibility in our humiliation.

Nowadays psychiatrists treat an array of patients who have no specific symptoms, but suffer from character and adjustment disorders, people now labeled "the worried well." But in those early days of therapy, with its much more restricted definition of mental illness, a mental patient always presented with a symptom. Some symptoms were clearly in the realm of the mental, although some might be products of an underlying physical cause, such as brain damage. An example would be the memory loss or personality changes that are manifest with certain brain tumors.

The first of the purely mental symptoms to be identified were obsessions, compulsions, phobias, delusions, and hallucinations. And common to all of these was the fact that they were subject to rational analysis, they had "meaning." They were not just random events. The awareness of an area of pathology that was in the mind rather than in an organ—the birth of mental illness—was the great transitional phase in the relatively new field of psychiatry.

One of the inquiries that served this transition, and will serve us in understanding scapegoating, was Freud's discovery of displacement. This emerged from his early attempt to understand the phobias that seem ubiquitous in children between the ages of three and five, in his celebrated study of Little Hans.* Displacement is an essential feature in the process of scapegoating, which is central to the psychology of the terrorist. The model established in this simple case of Little Hans is a paradigm for understanding the hatred that we see today.

Imagine the predicament of any five-year-old child beginning to establish his own identity by starting the process of loosening the bonds with his parents. He is terrified of his own anger with his parents and equally terrified by their potential responses,

*All citations from Freud are from *The Collected Works of Sigmund Freud*, standard ed. (London: Hogarth Press, 1955). Figures refer to volume numbers and page numbers in the above edition: 10:3.

should he make his anger manifest. What can he do with his defiant rage? There is no way to win a power struggle with the parents. The child knows he is smaller and vulnerable to their retaliation. He cannot win this battle. But the thought that he might win is even more frightening. The parents are the strong protectors needed to shield him from the dangers of a hostile and unpredictable world. A power struggle with the parents is always lost, particularly when the child is allowed to win.

The classic way of handling such aggressive impulses and the anxiety that ensues is to displace it to an imaginary figure, a ghost or a scary animal like a dray horse or a wolf. Animal displacements are particularly wonderful. All that is needed to control the anxiety is to avoid the source of danger. One cannot avoid one's father at this age, but how many wolves is a little boy likely to meet in his daily activities within his house? If the danger were with horses, the danger was outside. One could feel safe only at home. Ironically, this last statement summarizes the condition of most phobias. Displacement and avoidance are the defense mechanisms that are offered to explain all phobias. And phobics characteristically tend to remain—or retreat—to the safety of their homes.

The case of Little Hans was a landmark discussion of the general problem of how human beings attempt to handle the existential anxiety that is the inescapable product of the human condition. One normal way of handling our anxiety is to displace it. Direct it at some controllable cause, other than the true and inescapable one. This displacement is practiced by all of us in our daily activities. It is a central mechanism of bigotry and hatred. When the real oppressors are too terrifying or powerful to confront, find a safer population toward whom you can direct your hatred.

Freud utilized this and other cases to explain the formation of symptoms in general. He believed that analyzing the symptom would direct the physician to the underlying causes. He stated that each symptom contained a symbolic representation of both the cause of distress and the attempted resolution. He labeled symptoms "compromise formations," meaning that they were a compromise between a dangerous feeling and the defense against the impulse. The neurotic behavior was designed to protect ourselves or our standing in our own eyes. It is a model that lends itself to understanding aberrant social behavior as well as hysterical paralysis.

Some of these attempts to give specific meaning to a symptom became convoluted to the point of embarrassment. I remember once reading that a peptic ulcer was the product of "the bite of the introjected [swallowed up] mother." The fancifulness of some of these elaborations was a product of the ebullient enthusiasm of the early practitioners. Foolish as the elaborations were, they should not distract us from the recognition of the profound impact that these early studies of "disease" had on the everyday behavior of the well. Freud's genius did not lie in his conjecture that all behavior could be explained by his Libido theory. His great contribution was his assumption that *all behavior could be explained*! Starting with the most bizarre symptoms, the irrational delusions and rants of the madman, Freud took that which was the mark of madness—crazy, meaningless, irrational, purposeless lunatic meandering—and offered it up as scientific data to be evaluated seriously. If one starts with a symptom, one could locate a cause. Once the cause was discovered, one was on the way to a cure.

Over the years, certain early Freudian postulates were abandoned. But basic ones endured. Symptoms were still perceived as problem-solving devices. Symptoms were maneuvers designed to resolve painful dilemmas arising from many sources: perceived failures, cowardice, shame, impotence. They still had meaning, and they were still seen as failed attempts to ease psychic distress, that is, they were still seen as examples of the "cure" being worse than the disease.

The great psychoanalytic teacher Sandor Rado referred to a symptom as a "misguided repair." A symptom is an attempt to solve a problem, but it is misguided, since it does not really work. It will leave the patient worse off than he was in the life situation with the symptom he attempted to remedy. It is a plain term that I find useful.

In inventing "mental" illness—illness of the mind as distinguished from brain disease—Freud started a process that led him well beyond his roots in medicine and his therapeutic intentions. Mental illnesses appeared in "normal" people, not just lunatics, and the absolute breach that had existed between the two was closed. It was not long before the major leap was made to an awareness that psychic conflict influenced *all* human behavior, not just the abnormal.

This Freudian bombshell had fallout the extent and range of which could not possibly have been anticipated at the time. His basic theories derived from mental illness were insights that could be applied readily in analyzing all forms of social and political behavior, even as I do now in the analysis of hatred. The apparently crazy aspects of mental illness are only crazy when examined superficially. When exposed to dynamic evaluation, their purposes are exposed. The crazy behavior of suicide bombers can also be analyzed and demystified. By extension, we can use the same dynamic explanations used in mental illness to better understand the social phenomena of prejudice, bigotry, and hatred, all of which have psychological roots. Understanding them can help in dealing with them.

Freud himself started the process. Since the same psychodynamic principles that operate with the sick operate with the healthy, we can understand motivation, character formation, values, prejudices, taste, and lifestyle. We can apply psychodynamic understanding to the underpinnings of legitimate religions like Christianity or the more bizarre uses of religious convictions demonstrated by the Christian militias.*

Beyond understanding the individual in his normal and abnormal ways, the psychodynamic approach helps us understand the dynamics of group behavior.† Group identities can be analyzed like individual identity—we can discover which psychological factors lead an individual to join a right-wing Christian militia. With these Freudian insights, we can examine the individual as part of his group, religion, profession, national roots. We can understand how an individual who has not himself been personally humiliated can suffer the shame and humiliation of the group with which he identifies. This explains the confusing presence of privileged members of the upper classes in hate groups. The awareness that an individual can only be fully understood within the various milieus he occupies legitimates a psychological study of environments and institutions like the KKK or Al Qaeda.

The examination of cultural institutions in the light of Freudian theory gave birth to the field of psychoanalytic anthropology.‡ Cultural anthropologists could interpret the variety of differing cultural characteristics without resorting to genetic or racial assumptions. There is a varying amount of generosity and selfishness, aggression and passivity, trust and paranoia, in different populations. The average individual of a paranoid culture will become more paranoid than the average member of a trusting community.

---

*See, for example, S. Freud, *Character and Anal Erotism*, 9:167, or S. Freud, *The Future of an Illusion*, 21:3.

†See S. Freud, *Group Psychology and the Analysis of the Ego*, 19:93.

‡For example, S. Freud, *Totem and Taboo*, 13:1.

Religion was now fair game for analysis. Freud saw God as the product of man, not the other way around. The Bible was not revealed truth, or if it was, what it revealed was not God's will, but man's thinking processes.* Now that religions could be viewed as products of culture, rather than the instruments of the Lord, we could analyze the disparities between Judaism, Christianity, and Islam. We could explore their cultural differences, seeing where was the vulnerability for paranoia and hatred in each religion.

And finally, the rise and fall of civilization itself could be reevaluated. Civilization as a constraining influence on human passion became a final concern for Freud, ironically just prior to the rise of Hitler.†

The genie was out of the bottle; there was no getting it back in. Freudian theory became a tool for the biographer, the historian, the sociologist, and the anthropologist. Freud presented an alternative to the theological view of human nature supplied by religion and the purely economic explanation of human woes offered by Marxism. Social problems that seemed irrational were now subject to illumination via psychological analysis.

With this psychological perspective, the excesses of hatred, bigotry, and other forms of destructive human behavior could be liberated from genetic determinism (bad seed); economic determinism (class struggle); or theological explanation (the work of the devil). A new frame of reference was created. Perversity in human behavior could be traced to its psychic roots.

We are still free to accept genetic determinants of behavior—God or nature. We can also exploit economic and political insights, whether from a Hobbesian, Lockean, or Marxist perspective. But we can now enrich the mix by adding the psycho-

---

*S. Freud, *The Future of an Illusion*, 21:3.

†S. Freud, *Civilization and Its Discontents*, 21:59.

logical dimension. We can now examine such subjects as prejudice, bigotry, and hatred with a more complex set of variables, recognizing them for what they are: psychological symptoms of sick behavior.

8

THE PARANOID
SHIFT

The words "paranoia" and "paranoid" have made the journey from psychiatric lingo to common parlance. We hear them everywhere these days. In everyday language, these words suggest a person who is suspicious, distrustful, and ready to feel unappreciated, cheated, and betrayed. These are precisely the same attributes that the psychiatrist sees as the symptoms of the paranoid patient.

What has not followed in the transfer from the clinic to the marketplace is an understanding of the mechanisms of paranoia. The paranoid delusion—I am the agent of God; I am God—is one of the strangest of all symptoms, but one that is particularly useful in understanding the processes of hatred. For one thing, the delusion seems to defy all reason. It is so "crazy." At cursory examination it seems to offer no relief for the patient. Some paranoids express grandiose ideas that conform to the idea of a symptom as a coping mechanism. Grandiosity is an attempt to relieve humiliation, but how does one explain the delusions of persecution—

enemy aliens are beaming hateful accusations into my brain—that dominate the world of other paranoiacs and cause them abject misery? What purpose does this serve? How is paranoia a reparative maneuver, misguided or otherwise?

Since paranoid mechanisms are at the heart of the phenomenon of hatred, to appreciate what goes on in the minds of those who devote their life to hatred, we must understand paranoia. To get to that understanding, we can capitalize on the insights learned about symptom formation and the meaning of symptoms. Armed with the awareness that both hatred and paranoia are symptoms, we can look at the "symptom" of hatred as a misguided repair and try to locate the underlying conflict that the hatred attempts to accommodate.

The distortion that dominates paranoia is a quasi-delusional or delusional view of the world and one's place in it. The underlying cause that leads to the delusion is invariably a severely damaged and debased sense of self. To protect pride and face—to preserve self-esteem—the paranoid utilizes his imagination to find enemies on whom he can blame his desperate straits. He searches for a person or group on whom he can displace his rage and envy, similar to the way that the phobic displaces his anxiety. He ascribes the cause of his personal misery and failure to some manipulative and vindictive enemy, preferring to see himself as a victim rather than a failure. This assignment of responsibility for one's failure and misery away from oneself is called "projection" in psychoanalysis. I prefer the term "paranoid shift" for reasons that will follow.

Everyday Paranoia

Elements of paranoia probably exist in all of us, since it is a common derivative of that ubiquitous feeling of insecurity that plagues most of us in our competitive world. It is easily recognized by the associated feeling: "Isn't that just my luck!" Take, for example, the nagging and irrational feeling that many people experience at the supermarket, where it seems that whatever line they join at the checkout counters will inevitably be the slowest. Or on the highways when drivers engage in the compulsive, dangerous, and irrational lane shifting during a traffic jam, convinced somehow that their lane is always the slowest. They seem to be joined almost exactly by an equivalent number cutting in the opposite direction suffering from the same fear that they were trapped in the slowest lane. I have tried to track lane progress by stubbornly staying in my lane and marking for memory a car in the adjoining lane. I have rarely noticed any evidence of progress made by lane switching.

Most of us have on occasion suffered from the "just my luck" (always meaning bad luck) syndrome. I have watched the uneasiness of both friends and strangers who, on being led to a table by a maître d'hôtel, see in the assignment of tables some statement of respect or lack thereof. Being an early diner, I have been astonished by the significant number of people who refuse the first table offered. Diners will suggest the left side of the room when offered the right with almost the same degree of affirmation of their entitlements as those who choose the right side when offered a table on the left.

On the many trips I have made to Scotland, I have been appalled by my bad luck with the weather, since the natives always assure me how sunny it had been in the weeks before my arrival. Of course I know that it rains a lot in Scotland. Still, does every trip have to be a wet one? Yes, it does. Only after stumbling across the data in an almanac and discovering that in August, my month for travel, one can expect eighteen days of rain in Scotland, did I reluctantly give up my "bad luck" feelings.

The stock market, with its irrational vicissitudes, is another ideal locus for paranoid feelings. If I had waited, anticipated, held on, bought more, sold sooner, like—whom? Some unknowns who are presumed to have been wiser or luckier. It is the very possibility of winning—the upward mobility that promises so much—that feeds general feelings of exclusion from the ranks of the lucky. Those poor souls who deny statistics by buying lottery tickets beyond their means with the statement "someone has to win" refuse to accept the fact that, by definition, the one winner must be accompanied by hundreds of thousands of losers. One out of a million is the statistical equivalent of nobody winning.

In a competitive society such as ours, there will always be sources of anxiety and insecurity—a sense of entitlement unfulfilled—that can lead anyone to the occasional feeling of paranoia. But some people feel this all the time, in all manner of odd places. These are people who can be categorized as having a paranoid personality. Their paranoia defines their lifestyle.

The Paranoid Personality

At one time most psychiatrists drew a sharp distinction between neurosis and psychosis. The neurotic had difficulty adjusting to the real world. The psychotic was operating outside the real world. His perceptions of where he was and who he was were askew. We label this disorientation as to time, space, and identity a difficulty in reality testing and a hallmark of the psychotic. With the increasing awareness that we all are more inclined to credit the authenticity of the world of our perception than any actual world, the distinction between normal and psychotic has become somewhat obscured.

Strong elements of the paranoid psychotic are present in people who are said to have a paranoid personality. Nevertheless, when we talk of a "break" with reality, we mean that some border is crossed that transcends the normal distortions of perception. The psychotic may not know the date, the day of the week, or what century he is living in. He may not know whether he is in a hospital or a prison. And he may think he is Elvis Presley or Christ. There is a confusion of time, space, and person that introduces an element of the impossible into his thinking process.

Granted that none of us experiences reality directly. We all accept the distorted evidence of our perceptions as a true representation of the real world. Still, there is a difference between the normal boundaries of distortion and the gross break from reality required in delusion formation. Many a person obsessed with weight may feel fat when she is well within the borders of normalcy. But when an anorexic teenager who is hovering dangerously near emaciation and cachexia thinks she is fat, a line has been crossed into the area of delusional thinking. Similarly, the classic teenager who says to himself, "No one likes me," is profoundly different from the one who is certain that he is surrounded by a cadre of enemies acting in concert to destroy him.

The cultural level of distortion and the direction of that distortion differ remarkably. Some cultures set normal standards of wariness and suspicion that would be labeled paranoid in other cultures. Privacy standards vary within cultures. The threshold level of what is considered "normal" in an individual's behavior must account for the cultural standards under which he has been raised. Even with such similar countries as France and the United States, the level of openness and trust differ. The French view American openness as a sign of our ingenuousness. In contrast, Americans moving to Paris for business purposes are often shocked at the Frenchman's lack of hospitality. Executives are now often advised by industrial psychologists to be aware that an invitation to a French colleague's home is not as likely to be proffered as it might in the American Midwest. What Americans might view as aloofness would be judged as a proper sense of reserve by the French.

The line between more diverse cultures such as Afghanistan and the United States will be even more extreme. Whether a terrorist, or even a suicide bomber, may be considered mentally deranged will depend in great part on how far he has strayed from the norms defined by his culture. In a culture that will accept stoning a woman to death for infidelity, stoning an enemy's child to death may not seem so aberrant.

Further, the kind of an individual who will become a terrorist will differ from culture to culture. In the culture of modern America, we find a disproportionate number of psychotics among our homegrown, native terrorists. Optimism, a passion for life and the things of life, so dominates our society that when an American terrorist appears, like Ted Kaczynski—the infamous Unabomber who terrorized American academics in 1993—who turns his back on our culture, we are not surprised to find him a characteristic paranoid schizophrenic.

On the other hand, there seems little evidence that the terrorists who executed the 9/11 bombings were psychotic. They were probably not typical of the population from which they came, but their peers did not view them as deviant or sick. And the terrorists, prior to their suicidal acts, were not that different in their day-to-day behavior from the general population from which they emerged. They were students and civil servants, construction workers and professionals. There may have been some truly psychotic individuals among them, but the evidence at hand seems to suggest that the majority were not. They were, at worst, the paranoid extremes in a generally paranoid culture.

A paranoid population is not a population of paranoids. Rather, it is a group led by psychotic individuals who encourage paranoid elements endemic in the culture and in their individual personality. For example, the Turks who participated in the slaughter of the Armenians in 1915 could not have all been psychotic, any more than the Polish citizens of Jedwabne. We know that even

those who enthusiastically carried out the massacres of the innocents under Stalin, Hitler, and Pol Pot were not all psychotics.
Two brilliant, but somewhat contradictory, studies about the same
group of professional Nazi killing groups known as "Order Police"
insist on this very point, as is evidenced by the titles given to their
books: *Ordinary Men** and *Hitler's Willing Executioners.*†

The paranoid personality shares all the elements we will observe in the paranoid psychotic, while still holding onto a mod-
icum of reality, that is, without shattering his hold on a plausible
world. There have been many terms coined to characterize the
paranoid character, but they all tend to include the following
personality traits:

Negativism.   Paranoids display a negativism that underlies
their view of life and colors their expectations. This is an extension of the "just my luck" assumptions previously described.
Since attitudes influence judgments and expectations influence
outcomes, the "unluckiness" of the paranoid becomes a self-
fulfilling prophecy.

Suspicion.   Paranoids are universally suspicious and wary.
Since nothing good is ever expected, nothing new can be anticipated with joy or hope. Every unopened door leads to danger or
disaster; every messenger comes bearing bad news; every
stranger is a potential harm doer. The unknown is always a har-
binger for, and an extension of, the paranoid's familiar and expected feelings of deprivation. Hopelessness, being trapped in an
unrewarding environment, facilitates acts of desperation. The

---

*Christopher R. Browning, *Ordinary Men: Reserve Police Battalion 101 and the
Final Solution in Poland* (New York: HarperPerennial, 1992).

†Daniel J. Goldhagen, *Hitler's Willing Executioners: Ordinary Germans and the
Holocaust* (New York: Knopf, 1996).

abandonment of a life of frustration and humiliation is by definition less irrational than leaving one of hope and opportunity. If,
in addition, there is a certitude—an assurance by those who
know—that death is not a terminus, void, or end, but a portal to a
new and better life, even a reasonably rational person may elect
to become a suicide bomber.

Chronic Anger. Chronic anger becomes a way of life with
paranoids. The anger is not always expressed but can remain
dormant, awaiting an opportunity for excessive and often explosive expression. Rage, even misguided rage, is an empowering
emotion, particularly when it is used as a substitute for fear, guilt,
or shame. When rage is sustained over time, and when it is attached to an enemy who has been designated as the cause of
their misery, paranoids enter the realm of hatred.

Self-Referentiality. All paranoid personalities are extraordi-
narily self-referential, like their more seriously damaged counterparts, true paranoiacs. Group inconveniences or misfortunes
are always dismissed. Paranoiacs insistently focus their attention
on their own misfortune. Beyond seeing unfortunate events as
happening only to them, they see those events as happening because of them. A paranoid is enraged that *his* plane is always late,
never mind that everyone's plane is always late. The storms that
disrupt his travel plans are designed to deprive him. Even when
there is no tangible person to blame, simply the winds and the
rain, a metaphoric unnamed agent will be inferred.

Narcissism. A paranoid is the quintessential narcissist. It isn't
that it always rains on his parade—an indication of his bad luck.
Rather, it is that it rains *because* of his parade. This suggests that
he feels—even without the formulation of a delusion—that he has
been selected for misery by some unnamed and invisible forces.

At its extreme, these perceptions are referred to in psychiatry as "ideas of reference." The term is used in relation to a set of symptoms that are halfway to delusions. While not yet hearing voices, the paranoid with ideas of reference has the uncomfortable sense that people are looking at him, noticing him, or even closer to delusion, whispering about him. This explains the care with which New Yorkers avoid eye contact in close public spaces such as subways. "Whad'ya looking at?" from a paranoid stranger can be a prelude to an assault. In this context, looking is never interpreted as a glance of admiration, since the paranoid sees nothing in himself that others would admire. The paranoid personality's perspective always subsumes there is purpose and intent in all events, large or small, and the plan is always designed to deprive him, not just of goods, but of respect and love.

Paranoid Shift or "Projection."   Finally—and most crucial—a paranoid shift always occurs in paranoid thinking. I use this term as an alternative to the more ambiguous word "projection," which is the hallmark of paranoia. Projection is the process of attributing one's own impulses, feelings, or desires to others. The classic example is in Freud's attributing sexual jealousy to a projection of the jealous person's own desire to philander. Modern abnormal psychology places greater emphasis on the self, interpersonal relations, and adaptation than on instinct and impulse. In this frame of reference, it is more useful to see the paranoid mechanism in broader terms. It is not just our unconscious desire that we shift or project. It is the total responsibility for our failed existence that is transferred. In the process, rage supplants guilt.

The result of a paranoid shift is almost inevitably a conspiratorial view of life. "It"—whatever disaster or disgrace that stands for—didn't just happen, it was done to him. The paranoid always feels he is the victim of someone's machinations. He is denied promotion because he is old, obese, black, a Jew, not because he is less competent. The readiness to accept conspiracy theories in the modern American culture is a testament to the rising insecurity in our society.

Conjuring up a conspiracy is an alternative to being forced to accept the fragility of existence. It can extend, beyond paranoia, to relatively normal segments of the population. It relieves them of facing the randomness and chanciness of their own existence. It is too much to accept that something as precious as life can hang by a thread in the hands of a disinterested fate. Someone must be to blame for the tragedies that fill the evening newscasts. Accidental tragic events that arbitrarily choose one and spare another must be a product of some design or purpose. The randomness of life is a burden too great for many to endure.

Conspiracy theory demands enemies, thus completing the worldview of the paranoid. A tragedy does not just happen; someone makes it happen. And if they make it happen to us, they are by definition our enemies. All that remains is to locate the enemies and deal with them.

Grievance Collectors

The paranoid personality is sentenced by his own psychology to go through life with a constant sense of deprivation. Something to which he is entitled has been taken away from him. An actual state of material deprivation is not a necessary condition for paranoia or hatred. Since a feeling of deprivation goes well beyond material things, it will always at heart be seen as love and respect that has been denied.

Grievance collecting is a step on the journey to a full-blown paranoid psychosis. A grievance collector will move from the passive assumption of deprivation and low expectancy common to most paranoid personalities to a more aggressive mode. He will not endure passively his deprived state; he will occupy himself with accumulating evidence of his misfortunes and locating the sources. Grievance collectors are distrustful and provocative, convinced that they are always taken advantage of and given less than their fair share. They are often right. There is something about the defensiveness of the paranoid personality that invites just such behavior. People are more likely to treat them ungenerously and even unfairly in response to their churlish hostility. But even if they are not given less, they will perceive that which they have been given to be less. And they, like the rest of us, accept their perceptions as reality.

After a while they begin to seek out their own injustices. They are unhappy with success. Actual deprivation is preferred. It confirms their most profound and paranoid suspicions, thus confounding their critics. They have been accused of being paranoid—overly suspicious, cynical, and mistrusting; so be it. They will embrace this position. Each event in which they have been taken advantage of becomes a triumph for their bias. They are truly grievance collectors.

Underlying this philosophy is an undeviating comparative and competitive view of life. Everything is part of a zero-sum game. Deprivation can be felt in another person's abundance of good fortune. It is essential for the maintenance of the grievance collector's view of life not only to feel deprived but also to see evidence of his own deprivation in other people's good fortune. Envy is the accompaniment of his chronic state of anger. It supports and encourages it. All the evidence he so diligently collects only confirms that he is unfairly and inequitably served at every turn. Grievance collectors have constructed a world in which they choose to live where there are always winners and losers and they are always one of the losers. So, all winning diminishes them, and the only source of joy is schadenfreude.

It is my contention that it is never exclusively the deprivation of material goods to which grievance collectors are sensitive. The generosity of spirit and amiability that can be found in some of the poorest of cultures is tribute to the human spirit. Paranoids are sensitive to lack of respect, not lack of things. They are particularly sensitive to slights and abuses, which they see everywhere. They are constantly being diminished, or in modern terms, "disrespected."

Grievance collectors are the children of emotional poverty. So bruised and damaged is their self-esteem that they no longer hope for love, luck, or privilege. To hope for the good is to court disappointment and thereby compound their pain. To protect themselves from further disappointment, they anticipate the negative event. Traditionally, psychoanalysts have rooted such feelings of deprivation in a feeling of unlovability, a diminished sense of self-worth, fostered in early childhood. Many paranoids were indeed less-favored children. Family dynamics are complex. Some children are preferred to others for reasons that are not always apparent to outsiders. Compounding this felt injustice is the fact that all children raised with paranoid parents are likely to have paranoid tendencies. Children are more than ready to accept their parents' views of the world. A paranoid parental atmosphere, like an anxious one, is highly contagious.

This paranoid tendency can extend outward from the family and become the nucleus for a paranoid community. The paranoid community will then assure that the families within it have a culturally determined heavy dose of paranoia. Each enlargement from individual to family to community serves to lend greater and greater credibility to the paranoid ideation. Those who share the paranoid's environment now confirm the world as the hostile place that he perceives it to be. The Palestinian refugee camps are ideal environments for nurturing a paranoid view of life and a culture of hatred. Deprived of what they perceive as their proper homes by their enemies, the Jews, and unwelcome in the general populations of their "friends" in the Arab communities, the refugees are ripe for manipulation and exploitation.

For the most part, typical paranoids will not go through life in a constant state of overt rage. They will nurse their anger. They may even embrace it, living out their lives in a steady state of sullenness and anger with those others who may not yet be identified, but who have, by the paranoids' lights, deprived them of that which is rightfully theirs. They are like coiled springs waiting for opportunities to release the latent powers of their tension.

Paranoid ideation can thus be seen as being present in a spectrum from modest to severe, in this way no different from such character traits as generosity, affection, or narcissism. The final stage—the ultimate and most extreme expression of paranoid thinking—occurs in the fortunately rare form of a paranoid psychosis. The true paranoiac is the prototypic "lunatic," as expressed in popular literature and as perceived in the popular imagination. The condition is part of the recorded annals of almost all civilizations and is recognized in almost every culture as aberrant. The psychotic is a key player in the world of terror. And he must be distinguished from that antisocial menace, the psychopath.

9

THE PSYCHOTIC
AND
THE PSYCHOPATH

uman beings are unlikely to develop into either villains or
heroes. Nor are we for the most part psychotic or psychopathic. Most of us spend our lives living and acting in that
generously broad environment called normal. When confronted
with the rare extremes of human perversity, we are forced to re-
examine our attitudes about ourselves and our species. When we
are exposed to true evil, our first tendency is to turn away or explain away—to deny or rationalize. But true evil must be faced.
We must examine the acts of terrorism and try to understand the
kind of people who are prepared to commit them.

In this chapter I describe two sets of behavior that are beyond
the borders of normalcy, psychosis and psychopathic behavior.
Both are involved with hatred. These two behaviors are often
conflated because of the confusing terminology. They must be
differentiated. They represent entirely different conditions that

have different degrees of culpability and demand different forms of action.

I will not attempt to offer a definitive discussion of a paranoid psychosis here.* The appalling examples of hatred and human massacres witnessed in the past century and discussed in this book are not functions of rampaging madmen. Madness does not ordinarily lend itself to such organized behavior. It is the nature of the paranoid schizophrenic to avoid groups—not organize them. The purpose of discussing the paranoiac is that, as is often the case, it is easier to grasp the fundamentals of a condition at its extreme. The terrorists of Al Qaeda have been indoctrinated with paranoid ideas, but they are for the most part not psychotic. The individual, "self-employed" terrorist is usually a paranoid schizophrenic.

The Psychotic

Paranoia is the psychosis that is involved with acts of hatred. It is characterized by the formation of delusions and, in rare cases, hallucinations. The delusions fall into two seemingly contradictory categories: delusions of persecution and delusions of grandeur. A delusion is a false *belief* that entails an abandonment of all reality testing. A hallucination is a false *perception* often auditory—voices or radio messages from another planet—or visual

---

*The literature of paranoia is immense. For those interested in the psychology of paranoia, one of the more recent studies is Alistair Munro, *Delusional Disorder: Paranoia and Related Illnesses* (Cambridge: Cambridge University Press, 1999). An interesting fusion in "political psychology" can be found in Robert S. Robins and Jerrold M. Post, *Political Paranoia: The Psychopolitics of Hatred* (New Haven: Yale University Press, 1997). A brilliant fictional account of the descent into paranoia is found in Barry Unsworth, *Losing Nelson* (New York: Norton, 2000).

and tactile hallucination, as with the creeping insects that plague an alcoholic in delirium tremens.

While many hallucinations are chemically triggered, a delusion can still be understood in the same model used for lesser symptoms—as a coping mechanism, a misguided repair. A genetic predisposition, a chemical imbalance, and a dynamic explanation are not mutually exclusive mechanisms. As described previously in my analogy with music (see chapter 3), they must be viewed as different frames of references, different languages, brought to bear in an attempt to shed light and bring understanding to a complex human experience.

A psychotic delusion is one of the most bewildering and intriguing of symptoms. Grotesque as it may seem, it still subscribes to the general rule of a symptom as an attempt to control overwhelming anxiety. The repair is a costly one; delusions are the most destructive of symptoms, since they demand a true suspension of reality testing. To be certain that God is directing you to a specific mission of destroying known agents of the devil—or to actually believe that you *are* God—is to suspend belief in the real world beyond what normal self-deceptions require. Because this distortion in thinking is central to the various forms of schizophrenia, they have been referred to as thought (or thinking) disorders. Schizophrenia is one major subdivision of psychotic behavior. Affective (emotional) disorders, like depression, constitute the other category.

How could such bizarre ideation serve the purposes of daily life? It does so in the same way that avoidance serves the phobic. It offers a method of controlling, limiting, and rationalizing a free-floating and all-pervasive anxiety. Anxiety is the price we pay for the human capacity to anticipate the unknown future.

We tend to use words in everyday speech differently from the way psychiatrists use them. We say we feel anxious about an oral examination, job interview, or performance that is about to take place. Psychiatry would consider that worry. Psychiatrists distinguish anxiety from worry, reserving the latter for the emotion consequent to some impending and potentially dangerous event—a job interview, the need to enter a dark, enclosed space. Anxiety is reserved for a form of dread that has no immediately apparent stimulus. Since it exists without awareness of any threatening source or justification, it is labeled "free-floating anxiety." At one time or another most of us have experienced free-floating anxiety, an unknown dread that produces an edginess or even agitation.

Imagine a person, however, whose life is suffused with an overwhelming, constant, and pervasive free-floating anxiety. His life will be almost unmanageable. Here is where psychotic delusion formation may offer relief. If the psychotic makes the break from reality, he may delusionally decide, for example, that the person he most trusts, his mother, is not the person he thought she was, but an agent of his enemies. She is trying to poison him. This delusion rationalizes his anxiety. He is not crazy. It is logical and natural to feel frightened in the face of direct attempts on one's life.

In addition, the delusion universalizes his experience, thereby relieving his feelings of being strange or different; any rational person would feel anxious in these circumstances. Finally the symptom controls the anxiety by limiting its locus and focus. He need not feel anxious except when he is home and even then only when he is eating. He can control the anxiety by not eating the food prepared, or by taking precautions to make sure that his portions were not tampered with. This salvages time and energy to pursue his other normal activities. He controls the formerly all-pervasive anxiety by focusing it into one area of life rather than allowing it to spill over and contaminate all areas.

A delusion need not be simply the product of anxiety. It may be triggered by an immense rage, an overwhelming sense of shame and guilt, and what is most likely, an amalgam of all these emotions that leave the subject feeling impotent, helpless, and hopeless. This can produce the nightmare known as clinical depression, but in a person with a paranoid personality or a schizophrenic capacity to suspend reality, a delusional alternative is available.

The paranoid shift starts as a means of salvaging some self-respect out of humiliating circumstances. This shift allows the paranoid to view his misery as a product of the willful acts of some alien others. This shift allows the individual to view himself as a victim rather than a failure; guilt and fear are converted into rage, and shame is transformed into indignation. In the process, the individual is often transformed into a noble martyr chosen by God or some other higher source. It is this that links the delusions of persecution to the delusions of grandeur.

Sylvia Nasar in her biography of John Forbes Nash, Jr., a Nobel Prize winner in economics, presented an intriguing modern view of a paranoid schizophrenic.* The successful movie adapted from the remarkable book made the workings of the paranoid mind—and the ways in which they are first incorporated into and eventually become destructive of the person's life—understandable to a vast audience. Nash, a brilliant mathematician teaching at Princeton, was plagued with persecutory delusions, which led him to construct a complex view that placed him in a heroic struggle against evil, in which he was the secret agent of the CIA.

Freud's attention was drawn to paranoia by the publication of another remarkable book. In 1903, Daniel Paul Schreber, a former presiding judge of the appellate court in Dresden, Germany, published his autobiographical book, *Memoirs of a Neurotic*. Freud, not being an institutional psychiatrist, had little access to patients suffering from "dementia paranoids," the term then

---

*Sylvia Nasar, *A Beautiful Mind* (New York: Simon and Schuster, 1997).

used. Freud had certainly treated patients that by today's standards would be diagnosed as schizophrenics, but he tended to consider them as suffering from "hysteria" or "obsessional disorders." None of these patients had classical paranoid delusions; therefore, Freud based his pioneering and brilliant study of paranoia on Schreber's memoir.*

The parallels between the suffering of Schreber and that of Nash, separated by almost a century, reveal the power of good clinical observation and the ability of the paranoid mechanism to bridge time and culture. The differing details are reflections of the differing cultures from which the two men came. In general, nineteenth-century delusions like Schreber's were likely to stress God, spirits, and religion. The twentieth century substituted the powers of the state for that of religion, and invasive forces were less likely to come from Hell than from outer space. Whereas it was the CIA that was informing Nash, God, himself, directed Schreber.

Freud placed conflicts over what would later be defined as latent homosexual impulses at the heart of Schreber's psychosis. The illness, he postulated, was an attempt to control impulses that, in those days, and in this manner of man, would have been frighteningly humiliating. From this rather brief case, Freud illuminated the paranoid process and the relations and connecting links among (1) unconscious fears, humiliation, feelings of impotence; (2) ascribing these feelings to some identified enemies through projection; (3) delusions of persecution by those enemies; and finally (4) formation of delusions of grandeur. In this process weakness is converted into strength, degeneracy into honor, and shame into glory.

*Sigmund Freud, *Psycho-Analytic Notes upon an Autobiographical Account of a Case of Paranoia*, 12:3.

Many people today, examining Schreber's account, might choose to reject Freud's dynamic interpretation—the struggle against latent homosexual desires—ascribing quite different meanings to the same symptom. But Freud's description of the psychic maneuvers—the defense mechanisms—whereby the paranoid manages to salvage self-respect out of humiliation became a blueprint that guided generations of psychiatrists to an understanding of the seemingly grotesque and self-defeating ideations of their paranoid patients. These defensive maneuvers mirror the kind of cultural paranoia that has gripped many modern states. By insisting that symptoms have meanings, Freud encouraged taking seriously the rants and seeming gibberish of the psychotic patient.

It is significant that Schreber suffered his breakdowns in anticipation of elevation to a higher office. Classically, the stress of increased expectations or honors perceived as undeserved triggers episodes of decline. It is the anticipated humiliation, the public disclosure of inadequacy, that is dreaded. These days, the role of public humiliation is perceived as the common factor binding one paranoid fantasy to another.

Schreber went on to recover from his first illness rather quickly, but his second illness, some eight years later, became the subject of his extended autobiographical sketch. His earlier symptoms were "hypochondriacal ideas." But they were of such severity that we are likely these days to see them as delusional: He believed that he was dead and decomposing. Almost simultaneously, a paranoid shift occurred, and he saw these effects as something being done to him by his enemies rather than something happening to him through the unfortunate, but disinterested, course of disease. His physician from his first illness, a Dr. Flechsig, was responsible for this disease. Flechsig, as his tormentor, had now become a part of a more grandiose religious formulation, involving a struggle between God and the devil.

To transform one's daily miseries and humiliation into a symbol of a universal battle of the forces of good versus evil is only too reminiscent of the patriotic cry, "God is with us," that seems to accompany all wars. It is particularly prominent in the holy jihads pursued by the Muslim world today. Part of the human coping mechanism is an attempt to find purpose in the seemingly meaningless, and therefore unbearable, tragedies that befall us. Those who have a religious bent might comfort themselves over the loss of a child by viewing it as God's will and, as such, part of an inexplicable—since we are not delusional—grand design. However, religion itself would come to be viewed by Freud as a self-serving "illusion." Religious ideas were born from human needs to make an awareness of our fragile existential state seem less hopeless. That could be accomplished by converting life's inevitable end to a mere transition to a better world. Mortal creatures can become immortal by "discovering" an afterlife.

Schreber, after feeling maligned and persecuted, went on to the next step. He transformed his persecutory delusions into delusions of grandeur. The humiliating attempt to convert him into a woman, to emasculate him, was only an intermediary step to his becoming the redeemer of the human race. Rather than a humiliation, Schreber concluded that it was a sign that he had been chosen to be God's companion. He was no longer "the plaything of the devils" but an instrument of God's will. "He believed," Freud stated, "that he had a mission to redeem the world and to restore it to its lost state of bliss. This, however, he could only bring about if he were first transformed from a man into a woman." The physician then in charge of his case, a Dr. Weber, stated:

> It is not to be supposed that he *wishes* to be transformed into a woman; it is rather a question of a "must" based upon the order of things, which there is no possibility of his evading, much as he

would personally prefer to remain in his own honorable and masculine station in life. But neither he nor the rest of mankind can win back their immortality except by his being transformed into a woman . . . by means of divine miracles. He himself . . . is the only object upon which divine miracles are worked, and he is thus the most remarkable man who has ever lived upon earth.

Thus, that which started as a humiliation—his homosexual impulses—became a source of glory, a device to permit him to serve as the redeemer of the human race. The psychotic can, thus, be seen as confirming the rule that even the most outlandish and bizarre of symptoms must be understood as an example of misguided repair. He can live with his delusion better than he can with the constant torment that results from overwhelming anxiety from unrecognized sources.

In the earlier days of his illness, Schreber was "tortured to such a degree that he longed for death. He made repeated attempts at drowning himself in his bath, and asked to be given the 'cyanide of potassium that was intended for him.'" But as Weber noted, the "ingenious delusional structure" saved him from "insanity." By that he meant that the full-blown delusional system that ended in the redeemer fantasies freed Schreber and permitted him to return to "normalcy":

The fact was that, on the one hand, he had developed an ingenious delusional structure . . . on the other hand, his personality had been reconstructed and now showed itself, except for a few isolated disturbances, capable of meeting the demands of everyday life.

Dr. Schreber shows no signs of confusion or of psychical inhibition, nor is his intelligence noticeably impaired. His mind is collected, his memory is excellent, he has at his disposal a very considerable store of knowledge. And he is able to reproduce it in a connected train of thought. He takes an interest in following events in the world of politics, of science, and of art. . . . In spite of all this, however, the patient is full of ideas of pathological origin, which have formed themselves into a complete system, now more or less fixed and inaccessible to correction.*

During his second admission to a mental hospital, Schreber petitioned the courts to regain his liberty. "Such, indeed, were his acumen and the cogency of his logic that finally, and in spite of his being an acknowledged paranoiac, his efforts were crowned with success. In July 1902 Dr. Schreber's civil rights were restored."† Schreber, like Nash, continued his life outside an institution, clinging to his delusional system, and as far as the record shows, representing a threat to no one.

In the United States, bombers of innocent people are few in number and have tended to be psychotic. The most famous case in recent years was the previously mentioned Ted Kaczynski, the Unabomber.

Kaczynski's career as a bomber dated back to May 25, 1978, when he was known as the Junkyard Bomber because of the crudeness of his weapons. In a portent of what was to follow, the first bomb—while addressed to an academic scientist, a professor of engineering at Rensselaer Polytechnic Institute—was actually placed in the parking lot of the University of Chicago School of Engineering. A pattern of targeting research scientists was to emerge. This cycle of bombings ended in 1987 but was renewed

---

*Sigmund Freud, *Psycho-Analytic Notes upon an Autobiographical Account of a Case of Paranoia*, 12:12.

†Sigmund Freud, *Psycho-Analytic Notes upon an Autobiographical Account of a Case of Paranoia*, 12:30.

with new intensity and more sophisticated bombs in a cycle that began on June 18, 1993.

Kaczynski that day mailed two such parcels in what had become his signature trademark, a wooden box enclosed in a mailing envelope. One was addressed to University of California geneticist Charles Epstein. It exploded with such force that shrapnel was driven into Epstein's body and face, breaking an arm and obliterating three of his fingers. The second bomb was delivered to David Gelernter, a professor of computer sciences at Yale University. Gelernter barely survived and was severely crippled, losing most of his right hand.

Gelernter's brother was also a geneticist, which may be one reason David Gelernter was targeted. Certainly the focus for Luddite hysteria these days tends to be on genetics, partly because genetic research invokes the wrath associated with the issue of abortion, partly because molecular genetics operates at a level not easily understood by the layman, but mostly because genetics seems closest to the kind of "tampering" with nature that has traditionally (think of Dr. Frankenstein) frightened many with the fear of someone's "playing God."

What eventually emerged, when Kaczynski was finally apprehended through the courageous intervention of his brother, was the picture of a classic withdrawn and delusional schizophrenic living a hermit's life. In his delusional system, he perceived modern science as a force for evil, which justified his assault on its agents. The fact that he was schizophrenic meant that his assaults were disorganized, illogical, and irrationally executed. He seemed to attack at random those who were remotely connected to the offending sciences that endangered his barely articulated principles. He operated alone, as is characteristic of schizophrenics, who have a profound inability to relate to almost anyone. Like Schreber, he was primarily influenced by his own inner demons.

The psychotic individual may interpret events in life in a totally idiosyncratic manner—driven by his inner need to see things in a particular way—but he still will take his stimulus from the world around him. Except for the deteriorated schizophrenics of the back mental wards, most schizophrenics are not totally out of touch with reality. They are thus susceptible to the same influences as the rest of us. John Nash did work for the CIA, but in a mundane manner. Still he built his fantasies around his mathematical abilities and a romanticized need to be involved in the battle against evil represented by the Soviet Union during the Cold War.

Kaczynski was most likely aware of the battles over the possibility of human cloning, and for that reason for him genetics became the area of research in which the debate over the limits of scientific intervention in the human condition would be centered. He was, in addition, obsessed with computers. Methods of communicating have always been great source material for the delusional, particularly those that use invisible sources of energy with capacity to penetrate and influence—like radiation. Kaczynski, in his focus on computers, was in direct line with dozens of patients I saw in my early training who believed that "radio waves," "X rays," "television waves beamed from outer space" were means of either sending messages to them or taking control of them.

The real world may not appear the same to psychotics as it does to us, but the real world does influence them. Since anything can play into a preformed delusional system, schizophrenics can be the instruments, unintended or otherwise, of passionate and often overwrought single-cause advocates who see the whole world as secondary to their mission. In protecting the innocent unborn, passionate right-to-lifers have been prepared to take the life of the innocent mother. Animal rightists often seem willing to sacrifice researchers for rats, certainly for dogs or monkeys. But even if the more responsible members of those causes would not engage in such violence, their rhetoric suggests that they would, or it implies that to do so would be just and honorable. This rhetoric is ready tinder, waiting to ignite the psychotic, who is looking for legitimate explanations for his inner agonies and is eager to do battle against the evil that torments him. The inflated rhetoric of the radical fringe groups in the various rights movements supplies the rationalization that the psychotic needs and locates an enemy for him. He can now project his internal conflict to those who have been identified by others as threatening innocent populations or the world itself.

In May 2002, after the FBI had issued an all-points bulletin in relation to a serial bomber, Lucas John Helder, a twenty-one-year-old college student, was arrested. Cameron Helder, the defendant's father, said to reporters: "I really want you to know that Luke is not a dangerous person. I think he's just trying to make a statement about the way our government is run."*

By definition anyone who plants eighteen pipe bombs, injuring six people, is a dangerous person. If I were to ask the senior Helder, who knew of his son's actions when he issued his statement, whether he thought delivering pipe bombs into the mailboxes of innocent Americans was a dangerous action, I am reasonably sure that he would have answered yes. The father was in the same state of denial one encounters with other parents of dangerous children. And he was not alone. Even after all the evidence was assembled and published, Helder's friend said: "There's no way he could be armed and dangerous. That's just not him." His roommate and another acquaintance, a fellow member of the golf team, offered in Helder's defense the fact

---

*"Student, 21, Is Arrested in Nevada in 5-State Bombing Spree," *New York Times*, May 8, 2002, p. 1.

that "he never showed any emotion" even when he hit a bad golf shot, an observation that would be a red flag to any psychiatrist.

In support of a denial mechanism designed to protect us from painful realities, Cameron Helder did that which many liberal-minded individuals are wont to do: He attempted to separate the individual from his actions. He knew that the *inner* Lucas John Helder, his son, was a loving and decent boy. But there is no inner self that is separated from one's actions. Like it or not, what one does, one's behavior, is a better definition of the self than one's inner feelings. To probe for unconscious determinants of behavior and then define the person in those terms exclusively, ignoring his overt behavior, is a greater distortion than ignoring the unconscious completely. You, the essential you, will be better represented and understood through what you do than what you think.

But did the father even know what the son was thinking? In an attempt to explain his behavior, Lucas John Holder sent the *Badger Herald*, the University of Wisconsin's newspaper, a six-page letter, filled with chaotic statements about government, technology, and the environment. It included the following: "Do you wonder why you are here? Do you wonder what is out there . . . way out there? I remember those times of uncertainty, and I can't tell you how great it is to know, to know eternally, and to be."*

Much of his rhetoric and behavior suggests the psychotic: the sudden departure from his typical behavior; the discontinuity of actions from the stimuli that preceded them; the solitary nature of his behavior; his grandiosity and his exultation at the "great feeling" of liberation. All of this is more reminiscent of Schreber than of the organized hate groups that lynched blacks in the South, or the mobs of toughs that periodically go gay bashing, or

---

*Ibid., p. A22.

the psychopathic teenagers that set homeless people on fire as a form of entertainment. One would not be surprised to discover that evidence of prepsychotic conditions existed in this young man. Certainly when his father and friends said that he could not be dangerous, they were drawing on a history devoid of antisocial actions. His precipitous shift suggests a breakdown of traditional patterns, which is typical in a psychotic break.

During this same general period, England and Australia were also having problems with "mad bombers." These cases particularly expose the specific role of polemicists in stimulating even the most psychotic. The ultimate responsibility for crimes committed by many psychotics must be shared by those who inadvertently or directly manipulate them.

Glynn Harding, a twenty-seven-year-old patently schizophrenic man from Crewes, England,* sent dozens of potentially lethal mail bombs filled with nails and other forms of shrapnel in his defense of the rights of animals before he was apprehended. Psychotic bombers are notoriously difficult to apprehend. Their very irrationality contributes to this difficulty.

An article by Helen Carter in the *Guardian*, on September 22, 2001, took note of how tenuous was the association between Harding's animal rights beliefs and his selection of victims. Try making sense of this list—even as part of an animal rights crusade. Harding's first bomb was mailed to a firm that manufactured identity tags for farm animals. Successive bombs were sent to an agricultural real estate agent, a British Heart Foundation charity shop, a pet and reptile store, a sheep farmer, a cancer research charity shop, a poultry breeder, and a fish and chip shop.

---

*A psychiatrist cannot, or should not, make a psychiatric diagnosis on the basis of reportage. When someone is labeled a "schizophrenic" in this book, it is because that diagnosis has been made by experts who have examined him. Otherwise, I will indicate that I am speculating or dealing in probabilities.

The youngest victim was a six-year-old whose father earned his living clearing wasps' nests.

Nothing is more indicative of the fact that the victim is primarily a vessel to receive the internally manufactured hatred of the terrorist than the arbitrariness by which these victims were selected. Bombings like these are clearly hate crimes, but they have often been directed at people who are not actually members of the hated group. With Harding, the self-acclaimed animal rights crusader, his chosen victims were in no way connected with the use of animals for experimentation. Even when his crimes were directed at an animal research laboratory, the putative source of his anger, it would still not represent that which truly generated hate in Harding's heart. The cause selected is a convenience for internal rage evolving over a lifetime of perceived deprivations.

Similarly in the long-standing Serbian-Croatian conflict, the civilians killed were usually just innocent neighbors. The slaughter required the abandoning of personal history and current reality. Innocent victims were viewed in continuity with the earlier atrocities committed in previous wars by previous generations often unknown to them. The most bizarre and cruel aspect of the dissolution of Yugoslavia was that both Serbs and Croats managed to put aside their historic hatred and join in massacring their Bosnian Muslim neighbors. The traditional hatred was Christian against Christian. But in the chaos of the dissolution of Yugoslavia and the land grab that ensued, the Serbs managed to displace their hatred to the convenient Muslims. The result was the massacre at Srebrenica, which rivaled those of the Nazis. In the world of haters, all victims are fungible commodities.

A legitimate cause rarely generates the kind of hatred that sacrifices the innocent. Hatred works in the opposite direction. The "cause" does not generate the rage. The rage demands locating a cause. Resentment at one's lot in life—remembering that there need not be actual deprivation but psychological feelings of deprivation—generates a powerful rage that seeks a justifiable outlet. The animal rights movement and its heated rhetoric supplied Harding—a presumed animal lover, since there were many other causes available—with a convenient hook on which to hang the hate generated by his inner turmoil.

There was no doubt that Harding was a diagnosed schizophrenic. But the law, itself, is "schizophrenic" in dealing with heinous crimes committed by the psychotic. The judge, Elgan Edwards, called Harding's actions "pure evil," which raises question about moral judgments and moral responsibility with psychotic individuals. If a crime is obscene enough, if it offends public morality, there will be a tendency to refuse to acknowledge the nonculpability assigned to the insane under the definitions of the sick role. The easiest way to do that is to deny the presence of the illness. There is latitude in accepting the definitions, since criminal insanity and psychosis are not congruent terms. The presence of a delusional psychosis in a defendant is not sufficient to meet the standards of criminal insanity in most jurisdictions. That will demand, in addition to delusions, a proven inability to conform one's behavior to standards of right and wrong.

A case with an even more confusing amalgam of motivating factors is that of Colin George Dunstan, a forty-four-year-old Australian, who started his rampage of letter bombing in 1998—at least according to one psychiatrist's testimony—because of a psychotic depression after the breakup of his relationship with a coworker. But his twenty-eight letter bombs were sent to a variety of government agencies. While it is true that both he and his girlfriend worked for the Australian Taxation Office, he had a previous history of hatred, independent of any perceived abuses on the job. Since his trial, it has surfaced that he was linked to a right-wing antigovernment terrorist group, the Australian Nationalists'

Movement, one of whose leaders, Jack Van Tongeren, is serving an eighteen-year sentence for bombing five Chinese restaurants in Perth. Dunstan, I suspect, is closer to Timothy McVeigh, the Oklahoma City bomber, who exhibited fewer symptoms of psychosis, than to Kaczynski, who was almost a prototype of the schizophrenic. Hate crimes that seem crazy need not be the product of crazy people.

The general public overestimates the potential danger of psychotic patients. We tend to respond to the sight of deranged psychotic individuals with fear. This fear is sustained by the occasional act of irrational rage performed by a psychotic individual, often a street person. During the time I was writing this book, there were reports in the *New York Times* of a stabbing on a public bus; a woman being pushed in front of a moving train; threatening assaults on the streets by a homeless man with a club. All of these are probably attributable to psychotic individuals. And all of these wrongly contribute to a sense that acts of hatred, like suicide bombings, must be acts of madmen.

In a major urban area of some twenty million people, like New York City, where the number of deranged wandering the streets must run into the hundreds of thousands, what is truly amazing is how few acts of violence are committed by them, not how many. There are probably fewer acts of violence committed by the psychotics that walk among us than the number of violent acts of road rage committed by the "normal." Certainly fewer violent crimes are committed by the mentally ill than the acts of violence involving drugs, crime, and sex. In my years, admittedly few, of practicing in an institution, I was attacked by a patient only once and that was not by a psychotic. Most psychotics suffer internally and suffer in isolation.

The main danger with psychotics is that they are suggestible and manipulable. They are susceptible to the provocative language of extremists—the radical elements of the animal rights

group and the right-to-life groups seem to attract the most psychotics. These causes have been adopted by paranoid schizophrenics to liberate them from the isolation of their personal
demons. Finding affirmation in a group rationalizes their delusions, making them feel less crazy.

Although psychotics contribute to a very small segment of hate
crimes, the leaders of hate groups are unlikely to be psychotic.
Remember that the psychotic is a shattered individual who has a
tenuous hold on reality. He is obsessed and preoccupied with just
keeping himself together. He is a loner who eschews human contact. He can do harm to others, but for the most part he, himself,
is the greatest victim of his disease.

The psychopath, in contrast, is a manipulator and a user. He
perceives others as a predator views prey. Unhampered by a conscience or feelings of shame or guilt, he exploits people as instruments to serve his personal gratification. He is a con artist and a
grifter, a mugger and a rapist. While some acts of hatred are a
product of the blurred vision of the psychotic, more are products
of the distorted behavior of the psychopath.

The Psychopath

When we first moved to New York City from the less sophisticated environs of Ohio, my wife would read with anxiety the
headlines in the tabloids, to which we had not been previously
exposed. She would be particularly concerned with the group
that came under the heading: "Model Boy Kills Mother!" She
would ask me, as a budding psychiatrist, how that could happen.
I explained that by definition anybody who killed his mother was
not a "model boy." Invariably these model boys had evidenced
less than model behavior in their past. Most were psychopaths.

Hate groups are not societies of psychotic or borderline psychotic individuals. Their members are more likely to be people who have been labeled by psychiatrists as either psychopaths or sociopaths. The psychopath is a severely flawed individual who illogically, but rationally, has been excluded from the category of the mentally ill. Illogically, because the mental distortions of the psychopath are in many ways as extreme as those of the schizophrenic. Rationally, however, because society could not function if psychopaths were allowed the privileges of the sick role. Given the kind of damage to their personhood they evidence and the actions to which this may lead, psychopaths will constitute the majority of chronic criminals. They must be held accountable, so psychiatrists have considered them "abnormal," but not ill.

The psychopath is identified by the absence of a clearly defined moral system, one of the essential features that distinguishes Homo sapiens from lower animals. The psychopath is described as having no conscience mechanisms. Psychopaths operating without conscience or with severely limited ones are fairly prevalent, if not in our own lives, in the newspapers and television. They are found among the thugs who earn a living by knocking old ladies over the head with a lead pipe to get the meager contents of their purses; those who sell crack cocaine to indulge their penchant for the easy life; the corporate executives who in the face of negative research findings encourage the public to purchase carcinogenic substances like cigarettes; the Ponzi artists of Wall Street; the despots of the African states that starve their own people to accumulate Swiss bank accounts to support their decadent existences.

Obviously, "psychopathic," like "paranoid," is a term that represents a spectrum of people with varying degrees of pathology. The label indicates the presence and nature of the pathology, not necessarily the degree. Just as there are degrees of paranoia, there are degrees of psychopathy. When racism was rampant in the American South, not all racists became members of the Klan.

And when the Klan's battle against integration was clearly lost, not all of them remained as active and aggressively obsessed with hatred as the Eastview 13 Klavern in Birmingham, Alabama. Indeed, when the time came to make a "political statement" on Sunday morning, September 15, 1963, not all members of this Klavern would have had it in them to throw a dynamite bomb into the 16th Street Baptist Church, killing four innocent girls aged eleven to fourteen. The kind of hatred exemplified here, and the history of involvement in hate groups later revealed in the bombers, suggest that they fit the profile of psychopaths, evidenced through a lifetime of antisocial activities.

The term "psychopath" is usually reserved for the chronic criminal type who is incapable of seeing the wrong in what he does. Since he is incapable of feeling guilt or shame, he is equally incapable of displaying true remorse, even when it is to his advantage in a court of law. Unless psychopaths are consummate actors, as one finds in professional con men, their emotions ring false and hollow even in the eyes of the untrained jurors. But some are seductive and confident liars. Many people were reluctant to consider serial killer Theodore Bundy guilty of the murderous rampage, killing at least thirty-six women in the 1970s, in great part because of his physical attractiveness and easy manner.

The psychopath seeks opportunities to exercise his wanton cruelty and hatred. He pursues official activities that allow or call for the torture or humiliation of others. It is only the power of authority—sometimes a cult leader, but more disastrously, the state or organized religion—that can offer the psychopath a "legitimate" outlet for his unnatural impulses. The Birmingham, Alabama, bombers were likely psychopaths sanctioned by the perhaps less psychopathic characters of their racist colleagues, who applauded their behavior and protected them from early apprehension. The Germans—and the Lithuanians and Ukrainians—who *volunteered* to serve in the Nazi death camps were the counterparts of the street thugs who live by crime, and a great percentage of them were clearly psychopaths. One has to assume that they did not represent an authentic sample of those pressed into service by the Germans. But the Nazi Party did recruit a population of active psychopathic Jew haters into such legitimate state entities as the SS *Einsatzgruppen*, the killing corps that preceded the more efficient gas furnaces.

Some early students of human behavior perceived a human being as merely a sophisticated form of animal that, like the lower animals, is driven exclusively by hedonistic principles, that is, the desire to avoid pain and seek pleasure. The psychopath certainly operates in this manner, but he is not a normal human being.

Psychopathy is a developmental defect. We must not honor psychopathic behavior by seeing it as a natural extension of human drives. Most human beings are not driven exclusively by appetite and selfishness. We have ample evidence that survival and pleasure are decidedly not the only forces motivating humankind. A better case can be made for the potential within all of us for self-sacrificing actions.

Danger is great in times of war and disaster, yet acts of incredible courage are particularly manifest in these very situations. What motivates the soldier who hurls his body onto a grenade to save his comrades; the fireman who enters a blazing building to save a child; the captain who goes down with his ship after evacuating his passengers and crew? To explain such phenomena requires a more complex view of the human being than that of a survival-driven machine. In that great American classic, *The Red Badge of Courage*, the young nameless hero who had previously abandoned his comrades and fled the field of battle discovered courage:

> He suddenly lost concern for himself, and forgot to look at a
> menacing fate. He became not a man but a member. He felt that

something of which he was a part—a regiment, an army, a cause, or a country—was in a crisis. He was welded into a common personality which was dominated by a single desire. For moments he could not flee no more than a little finger can commit a revolution from a hand.*

For most people, inborn beliefs shape conduct, and ideals like courage, generosity, honor, pride, patriotism, responsibility, charity, compassion, and empathy set standards for behavior. We do not always have the courage or strength to achieve our ideals, but when we abandon them, our conscience inflicts its toll for cowardice or weakness. Failing our internal principles produces the emotions of guilt and shame. These are as powerful elements in shaping normal human behavior as fear and rage; some would say they have greater motivating force. The agonies of guilt and shame make us pay a severe price for failing our ego ideal and perhaps prepare us for doing better in the future—that is, *if* we experience these emotions and *if* we perceive a future. The psychopath is capable of neither.

Characteristically, the psychopath is incapable of feeling either shame or guilt. He feels no contrition. Compounding this is a distorted sense of the future. He really may be perceived as denying the future. The psychopath grandiosely assumes that he will prevail without facing any punishment for his actions. Since it is only the present that he comprehends, he lives almost exclusively in the here and now, grabbing for instant gratification. Devoid of conscience, absent the emotions of guilt and shame, he pursues his own interests exclusively. The psychopath, driven by his personal survival needs, is motivated by the only emotions that operate within him: lust, greed, fear, and rage. He is effectively operating with the consciousness, and under the rules, that

*Stephen Crane, *The Red Badge of Courage* (New York: Norton, 1976), p. 30.

guide animal behavior. But he does not have the instinctual apparatus supplied to animals as an alternative to conscience. He will do that which higher primates would not, destroy children and the helpless, under the constricting influences of instinct.

While the psychopath can join a group, he has no capacity to identify with a larger group and feels no common purpose unless that purpose is the shared privilege of venting one's hatred. The psychopath uses such groups only opportunistically. In the blood sport of killing, he may temporarily find an exhilarating sense of the power of the group. After the lynching, the mob will dissipate and deconstruct into its isolated and disparate individuals like the spent pieces of an old jigsaw puzzle. The psychopath certainly cannot identify with any principle or ideal that involves others except for hatred.

Explanations of the cause of psychopathy have undergone radical shifts over the centuries. In the nineteenth century, Richard L. Dugdale proposed that psychopathy was hereditary, coining the term "hereditary psychopath." The two words became so intertwined that the term "psychopath" was eventually abandoned by many once Dugdale's work was refuted. "Sociopath" was substituted. Unfortunately, Dugdale, the eugenics movement, and the use of eugenics to support Nazi racial theories were the final nails in the coffin, making any legitimate examination of genetic influences on behavior suspect.

Does it really matter whether psychopaths are born or made? They wreak their havoc anyway. When one sees them as agents of evil, how they are made becomes less important. But it certainly matters in the therapeutic and prophylactic world. We must also face up to the fact that a culture may encourage and support psychopathic behavior. It can bring out the paranoid elements of more normal populations. The psychopath is at his most dangerous when he possesses the intellect, the charisma, and the opportunity to fire up larger populations. We know that deceptive psychopaths have taken over large corporations and large nations.

Even when the psychopath does not possess those character traits that open the door to leadership, he can become the hit man, the torturer, or the executor of the policies of the leadership. The danger of the psychopath is compounded when he finds support in a culture of hatred. Then he becomes the agent of the resentments and frustrations, the humiliations and despair of that larger group. He will lead the Klan and run the furnaces at the Nazi death camps and encourage acts of terrorism.

It is sometimes difficult to distinguish the psychotic from the psychopathic. The pure schizophrenic is the easy case. There was a pathetic quality in the schizophrenic demeanor of Lucas Helder—with his serious attempt to create a pattern of "funny faces" out of the bombing sites—that was in sharp contrast to the cold, unyielding, and psychopathic hatred of Timothy McVeigh.

But the extreme psychopath is hard to distinguish from the psychotic, since almost all psychopaths display the marked paranoid traits that are the hallmarks of the paranoid schizophrenic. The organizational abilities and the people skills of Hitler suggest the psychopathic rather than the psychotic. And then there was the fact that the Germans almost universally adored him, actually found him charming. The author and reviewer Naomi Bliven expressed incredulity that the Germans "found charm in a man who gobbled sweets, made disgusting comments on food at the table, engaged in staring matches, bragged about his intelligence, and flew into a rage when anybody questioned one of his statements."* She inferred that their love of Hitler revealed some idiosyncrasy of the Germans themselves.

---

*Naomi Bliven, review of *The Psychopathic God: Adolf Hitler*, by Robert Waite, *New Yorker*, August 29, 1977, p. 84.

With Stalin, the call is more difficult. He was universally distrusted and hated. With his readiness to locate enemies everywhere and in every population, he may well have been psychotic, although with his well-honed instincts for self-protection, I am likely to include him among the psychopaths. The behavior of such people as Idi Amin and Pol Pot, even when out of power, certainly suggest the psychopath. The evidence seems clear that the major despots of hatred are primarily psychopaths. Still, both psychotics and psychopaths represent the minority of those who kill with hatred.

When considering the torturers, the leaders of the death camps, the various executors of the policies of the governments of hate, we are certainly not dealing with the insane. Some of them, particularly those who volunteer for torture and murder positions, are clearly psychopaths, that is, lucid thinkers with no moral compass. But the most frightening fact is that horrifying mass crimes of hatred are endorsed, supported, and ultimately acted out by "normal" members of the population.

The "ordinary men" of Reserve Police Battalion 101 carried out a massacre of Jewish mothers and children at Jozefow, Poland, on July 12, 1942. Only a dozen of the 500 police had accepted the offer of a senior officer to be excused from the killing. The effect of the slaughter on the murderers was at first "shattering." Part of their problem was their lack of experience. In the opening days of the slaughter, they shot freehand at point-blank range. As a result, "the bullet struck the head of the victim at such a trajectory that often the entire skull or at least the entire rear skullcap was torn off, and blood, bone splinters, and brains sprayed everywhere and besmirched the shooters."* This put severe emotional

---

*Christopher R. Browning, *Ordinary Men: Reserve Police Battalion 101 and the Final Solution in Poland* (New York: HarperPerennial, 1992), p. 64.

stress on the men. One said, "I thought I'd go crazy if I had to do that again."* So some changes were made in the procedures. With time and conditioning, the men continued their massacres, and, remarkably, they did not go crazy. They adjusted.

The level of hatred in our modern world is appalling, and the cultures of hatred seem ubiquitous. They are not the products of the deranged. The slaughters in Rwanda and the Sudan—like the destruction of the Armenians by the Turks and the massacre of the Jewish population of Europe by the Nazis—were discharged not by psychotics and psychopaths but by normal members of the population. Not by delusional madmen and conscience-free brutes, but by people like you and me. How does one explain the forces that allow populations of normal people to experience such abhorrence and express such malignant hatred toward other populations of normal people? Here one must look, not to the pathologies of the mind, but to the normal phenomena of group identity and cultural animosities. Here we leave the area of hatred as an emotion and enter the domain of hatred as an attachment.

---

*Ibid., p. 76.

HATRED

AS AN
ATTACHMENT

10

IDENTIFYING
THE SELF

Human development—the process by which people emerge from childhood to become the diverse kind of adults we observe—has occupied students of human nature for centuries. Before the emergence of the social sciences, human development was most eloquently, though elliptically, described in literature. Such writers as Dickens, Stendhal, Balzac, Tolstoi, and Twain gave a literary testament to Wordsworth's assertion that "the child is father of the man."

Why people behave differently—adopt different values, measure themselves by different standards, embrace aggressiveness or conciliation—has traditionally been attributed to genetic endowment or environmental impact, depending on the biases of the culture. The evidence strongly suggests that overemphasizing either to the detriment of the other is an invitation to disaster.

In the Soviet Union under Stalin the strange concept of equality adopted by the Communists demanded that all children be seen as born with equal potential. The Stalinists' insistence on

this posture led them to deny even the basic Mendelian principles of genetics in all plants and animals. They were reluctant to
accept the proven fact that inheritable traits influence all life.
They denied the very existence of inherited genetic traits. Instead, they adopted a pseudoscientific "genetics"—called Lysenkoism after its founder, T. D. Lysenko—that better suited the
egalitarianism of Marxist ideology. The stubborn adherence to
Lysenkoism—denying genetic inheritance while insisting that ac-
quired characteristics could be transmitted—eventually destroyed
Soviet agriculture and contributed to the massive starvation that
was endemic under Stalin's rule.

Even open societies have had difficulty accommodating to the
fact that genetics plays a part in human development and variability. The tragic and distorted use of genetic theory by the
Nazis caused liberal communities to reject the possibility of genetic differences in human potential. Humanistic democracies
want to believe that any child can grow up to be a Beethoven or
a Newton. The rapid evolution of the understanding of genetics
in the past fifty years, however, has forced an awareness of the
importance of genetics in determining at least some aspects of
human conduct and character. Still, in the area that concerns
us—not extraordinary talent or genius, but mere fulfilling of natural human patterns—the weight of the evidence clearly attests to
environmental factors in human development. As such, the
moral character of the child is hostage to the quality of parenting
and the values of the culture.

Although the need for some community is a fixed part of our
biology—we are obligate social animals—the quality and characteristics of these communities are not dictated by nature, as is the
case with animals. Given human flexibility and autonomy, the
kind of social environments we create can vary dramatically. As a
result we have developed such paranoid cultures as the Yano-

mamo Indians of southern Venezuela,* the Albanians under the
Communists, and the shrouded enigma that is North Korea.

In our concern for individual hatred and cultures that encourage hatred, we must address human development at least minimally. Since hatred—beyond being an emotion and a thinking
disorder—is a pathological attachment of one person to another,
we must examine the nature of attachments. We must follow the
trail from the first identification of a self; distinguishing ourselves
from others; attaching ourselves to others; and, finally, identifying with those to whom we are attached. In this process we find
allies, build communities, and ultimately locate enemies.

Identity: The Self

How do we first discover our "self"? Before even differentiating
the me from the you, how do we distinguish the me from the
inanimate things around us, the blanket or the diaper? No one
can peer inside the mind of the neonate and precisely determine
what thoughts exist there. Nonetheless, we have learned to com-
municate quite well with infants. Researchers have found ingenious ways to determine the likes of a newborn and by inference
something about his perceptions. Newborns have variable sucking rates, for example. If we reward fast sucking, the newborn
will signal for that reward by sucking fast. In this way we learn
what rewards are preferred by the neonate. To our amazement, it
turns out that certain newborns will indicate that they prefer
light shows, that is, visual stimulation, to sound shows. A minor-

---

*See Napoleon Chagnon, *Yanomamo: The Fierce People* (New York: Holt, Rine-
hart and Winston, 1968).

ity of neonates prefers the sound shows. And this latter group, when followed into maturity, seems to produce more children with dyslexic problems.

Brilliant new sonar technologies suggest that the late-stage fetus is more aware than we had previously thought. But aware of what? Certainly not of himself versus the surrounding amniotic fluid in which he floats or the placenta to which he is attached. And certainly not to the mother who carries him within her body.

Most theories that have emerged from developmental psychology suggest that the earliest consciousness of the neonate is an awareness of a self and nothing but a self. In other words, the problem is not self-discovery, but world discovery. Many fanciful phrases have been applied to this period, such as the stage of "primary narcissism" and the age of "magical omnipotence." The reasoning behind these assumptions is based on the knowledge that before the neonate has any true perception, he experiences sensations. Some see the first sensations as occurring around the mouth during the feeding experience that dominates early life. Others place the first sensations as tactile, noticing that with dogs, the process of urination, essential to survival, will not be initiated without perineal licking and stimulation by the mother.

Still others see the first sensation as the proprioceptive senses. These are the awareness of body parts experienced in the stretching and contracting of muscles. We do often sense "ourselves" in adult life through the positions of our body parts in relation to each other. To know where we end certainly means that we know where something else begins.

At any rate, sensations precede emotions, and both precede ideas. We know that a child responds to pinpricks, wetness, and hunger. But what do we mean when we say that the baby is hungry? The "concept" of hunger can't yet exist. All that he is aware of are the gastrointestinal hunger pains. He screams in a special way different from the distress of sleepiness. Is that rage? It is hard to tell. If it is, a case can be made for a very early consanguinity between deprivation and rage. Most parents, recognizing the cry as a plea for food, supply it and assume the baby is "asking" to be fed. Some parents assume all cries to be requests for food, and we are on our way toward an obese child.

Then what happens? The infant cannot possibly understand the complex chain of events that result from the cry: If the father awakens first, he will more often than not nudge the somnolent mother to prepare the bottle or commence nursing. The infant's cry should not be perceived as a wake-up call. He cannot possibly be aware of this as a form of communication. This has led to the assumption that he views the screaming itself as leading directly to the suffusion of the warm liquid that alleviates the distress. I seem to remember as my first memory the feeling that, when lying in the dark in a crib, I could make it become light by simply opening my eyes. As though no time elapsed, but the presence of dark and light were results of my closing and opening my eyes. No sense of day and night as phenomena independent of me and my actions was yet present. This presumed sense of one's own self alone, and in control of one's needs, leads to the assumption that the earliest stage of childhood is one of magical omnipotence. The child is aware of only an isolated and powerful self.

Soon the child learns differently. He begins to perceive an alien environment out there that is essential for his survival, but that seems indifferent or unresponsive to his needs. With that he discovers his own impotence. He can do nothing for himself. He is helpless and dependent. In his mind he has been reduced from the all-powerful to the least fit. Oh, how the mighty has fallen! Despair could be the result. Some early psychoanalysts, Melanie Klein in particular, assumed that there is a normal period of childhood depression during the phase when the child reaches such awareness.

This sense of helplessness is quickly mitigated by the awareness that there are others out there who are strong and can take care of him. The child discovers his caretakers. The first differentiated figure is usually the mother. While the sense of his helplessness is slowly becoming apparent, the perception of her extraordinary power is magnified. In relation to the limited needs of an infant, the mother has godlike powers to satisfy them all. Through this transfer of powers from the self to the other, the infant has unearthed some immense realities that will influence him for the rest of his life: Despite our own limited powers, there are others who can take care of us; one can survive through dependency; others are essential for our survival.

With time, the child learns that the parents have the power not only to give services but also to withhold them. It is in this discriminatory behavior of the parents that the child discovers his relationship to authority. The child learns that parental willingness to care for him is related to the nature of their feelings for him. If they love and approve, they will tend to him. If they are angered and disapprove, they will withhold or even punish. The need to ingratiate the parents—and later all authority figures—will be perceived as an essential, life-and-death matter. We know our helplessness and we exaggerate their power. The child will strive, at least at first, to do that which the parents want. This means subscribing to their values. If generosity pleases them, we will be generous; if selfish pursuit of success is their aim, that will be our original goal.

This concession may seem like further humiliation, but it is truly empowering, for now our fate is back in our own hands. Pleasing the powerful is the next best thing to being powerful. Later the concept of an all-powerful God may emerge, one who can fill the gap left by the growing recognition of the inadequacies of our parents. This gives further evidence to the immense power that invoking "God's will" can have in motivating human behavior.

What has developed is the sense of an incomplete self that is a part of a community of supporting others whom we may influence. As the child develops, he takes the attitudes and lessons he learned in the family and applies this understanding in building new attachments. He makes friends—and enemies. He finds alternative parental figures in siblings, teachers, religious or political leaders. He builds networks and joins communities. He identifies with heroes other than his parents and with communities other than the family. He becomes a social human being. And all of these new identities and attachments influence his values and modify his perceptions and behavior. His community establishes his standards, sets his goals, and defines his conduct. And finally, his religious community will set the ultimate judgment on his moral worth.

In nineteenth- and twentieth-century Irish families, religious service was a respected tradition. Many families assumed one son would become a priest and one daughter a nun—and often they did. It was a matter of family pride to have a "religious" in the family. It is horrifying to realize that there are religions that may define "religious service" broadly enough to include blowing oneself up while taking as many "enemies" as you can along with you. But when that is the cultural definition of religious service, there will be a multitude of suicide bombers willing to do it and proud families to support it. Certainly, you would not expect a suicide bomber in every family, because that which is required is not a way of life, but death. Still, if the family life is squalid and unrewarding, and if the religion, as in some current Islamic jurisdictions, promises an afterlife rich in the material goods that are denied on earth today, a sufficient number of suicide bombers will be located to serve both the religious and the political agendas.

Since early nurture differs among individuals both qualitatively and quantitatively, the strength of the self varies. There are parents who beat, neglect, or brutalize their children. If the deprivation is sufficiently severe, the child will not survive. Or if he survives, what may emerge is an adult who is deficient in those very humane qualities that shape humankind. The child who is deprived of the proper care to which he is entitled may become an adult incapable of caring for others. It is likely that early scarring, more than genes, destroys the conscience mechanism and produces the psychopaths of our world. Guilt, shame, pride, and love are attributes inherently built into the human organism, but they must be nurtured to grow and survive.

Modeling and Identification

Human behavior is not merely a struggle for survival, a battle to avoid destruction. There are powerful positive motivating forces that serve other interests beyond survival, like ideals and pride. To understand both the positive and negative influences on character development, one must understand identification and modeling. Both shape behavior but do it through different pathways. In a discussion of hatred, this distinction is crucial. Heroes set standards for the rest of the population. They are models to emulate. One martyr will lead to another.

Identification—the process of fusing one's personality with a person or a group—determines our essential character traits, how loving and compassionate or resentful and paranoid we may eventually become as adults. Identification is central in deciding both whom we choose to love and whom we decide to hate and how inclusive each group will be.

Modeling refers to the child's consciously attempted mimicry of his parents, and later of other idealized figures, in a conscious effort to conform to their standards and gain their approval. We are most likely to choose as models those who seem most powerful, and to the young child it is always the parent. That will change with adolescence, as every parent knows only too well. In a strictly behaviorist model, the child responds to rewards and punishments. Some of these are explicitly stated by the parents. But parents are generally unaware of the degree to which tacit clues will equally be followed by the child. Parental facial expressions and their body language will influence the child's behavior more than specific injunctions. When an annoyed parent says, "Do what you want," she is really saying, "Do what I want, which I have clearly indicated in one way or another." Even the child's syntax, tone, inflections, and speech patterns are borrowed from the parents, which is why family members tend to resemble each other in more ways than just the physical.

What most likely happens is that the typical child randomly tests the parents with a variety of behaviors intended to gain their love and approval. If through trial and error the child finds that being cute, charming, and cuddly evokes a positive response or brings forgiveness for transgressions, he will use those methods more and more. If, on the other hand, the parent responds to the ingratiating behavior with distaste because he cannot tolerate it, the child will find an alternative path to approval. The way to this parent's heart may be through self-sufficiency—being a good boy, with everything that implies.

These two types of children will grow up to be different. One will see performance and achievement rather than ingratiation as the primary means for gaining approval. He will see action rather than accommodation as the way to approval. Each will tend more and more to use the successful methods. Children are masters at reading their parents' moods. They have to be. Their lives—at least in their distorted perceptions—depend on it. But a child operates in other ways that are independent of trial and error. A child shapes conduct through mimicry and imitation, using the devices of both modeling and identification.

Fortunately, or unfortunately, we are not limited in our modeling to the parental figures alone. Older siblings often serve as models. In later life we can identify with teachers, mentors, friends, and public heroes. One's identity is therefore an amalgam. It will involve conscious modeling of these icons, where certain traits are scrupulously copied and others just as avidly eschewed. But we may not be as much in control as we would like to believe. We may discover ourselves in adult life—often to our chagrin—behaving precisely the way our parents behaved, and in fashions that previously embarrassed or humiliated us.

Conscious modeling is generally most effective only in less important aspects of life. We can reject the European or Midwestern cadences with which we were raised, substituting the tonier Eastern accents of our classmates or teachers, or for that matter, the ghetto-speak that seems cooler. We can tailor our clothes and cut our hair to whatever pattern is de rigeur for our generation. But most of what drives behavior in crucial areas will have been established earlier in life through less voluntary and rational means.

Modeling has minimal influence compared with the power of the automatic identification that goes on willy-nilly even when the child assumes he is rejecting the parental directives. Identification is a peculiar process. It operates on an unconscious and involuntary basis. A mother is likely to influence the design of her child through those areas of her behavior over which she, herself, has little or no conscious control. In governing the nature of her offspring, what she *is* will be more a determinant than what she *wants*. This concept of identification is so powerful that it mystifies parents, who are unaware of the distinctions between their instructions and their actions. A little girl will often behave as her mother wants her to behave out of fear of her mother or love for her. But that same little girl will behave like her mother—even if that may not be the way the mother wants her to behave—out of a strong and almost automatic process of identification. When a girl starts talking like her mother, employing her inflections and tonality, when she starts demonstrating the same walk and body language, it is not a conscious act of imitation. It just happens. It is a reflection of identification.

Identification is the most powerful of the behavior-determining forces.* Most things are learned piecemeal, one at a time, through trial and error. With identification we learn automatically and with a "wholesale" adoption of the forms, habits, and even the values of the parents and the culture that shaped them. Through identification, we psychologically swallow up the parent—called "introjection" in psychoanalysis—and fuse his or her identity with our own. In this way we adopt behavioral patterns in big, indiscriminate blocks by incorporating the character and identity of others.

Identification, however, does not mean that we cannot reject aspects of our parents' personalities. Rebellion and self-assertion are also a part of the growing-up process. In an elementary school every child "votes" the way his parents do. By high school one will find Democratic children of Republican parents, indicating both adolescent revolt and independent thinking. When a child insists on behaving in complete opposition to his parents, the behavior is a perverse form of dependency. Dependence can be expressed in defiance as well as obedience. When a child does something just because her parent objects, the parent is still the determinant in her behavior.

For the most part, even after allowing for rebellion and true independence, we retain more of the parents within us than we like to admit. This helps to explain the "hereditary" nature of personality—why Japanese children tend to grow up and behave

---

*Identification was most completely explored in the works of Erik Erikson. The best introduction for the layperson is still Erik Erikson, *Childhood and Society* (New York: W. W. Norton, 1963).

like Japanese, whereas Swedish children persist in behaving like Swedes. It certainly explains the culture shock many of us feel on first being exposed to a culture significantly different from our own.

When we identify in this way, we are not only likely to talk, walk, dress in the manner of those with whom we have identified, but of more significance, we will tend to reason and think like them. We adopt not only the manners but also the mind-set of those with whom we identify, and we do it wholesale.

An admiration for certain traits sets a standard for a revulsion against others. Almost a century after the great massacres, Armenians—whose grandparents may have only known about the tragedy from second-hand sources—harbor an intrinsic distrust, even hatred, of the Turks. I am not offering this phenomenon as a universal finding, but its persistence even fractionally in a population four or five generations removed from the event is a tribute to the powers of identification.

The 2002 Nobel laureate in literature, Imre Kertesz, said in an interview: "My Judaism is very problematic. I am a nonbelieving Jew. Yet as a Jew I was taken to Auschwitz, as a Jew I was in the death camps and as a Jew I live in a society that does not like Jews." He felt that to a large extent his Jewishness was "imposed" on him. Still, when he visited Israel, he was surprised by the power of his identification: "I am not impartial and, moreover, cannot be. I have never assumed the role of impartial executioner. I leave that to European—and non-European—intellectuals who embrace this role for better and often for worse. They have never bought a ticket for a bus ride from Jerusalem to Haifa."*

---

*Alan Riding, "Literature Nobel Awarded to Hungarian Writer Who Survived Nazi Death Camps," *New York Times*, October 11, 2002, p. A8.

The power of identification places a great burden on the leadership of major populations, whether on the national or religious scene. Group identification often depends upon the existence of an other, an outside, nonbelonging population. By setting an alien population outside the moral community, the leaders lay the groundwork for possible stigmatization and demonization of the other. The hatred of the Serbs for the Croats was inflamed by the active cooperation of the Croats with the Nazis. But the hostility between these two groups extended back to the Byzantine world, which separated the Greek Orthodox from the Roman Catholics. Since the split dates from the synod of Photius in 867 A.D., it is centuries before the life and personal memory of any living relatives. This hostility had to be abetted by the attitudes of the churches themselves, which have a longer memory for differences than for shared ideals. Certainly nothing was done within the institutions of the two churches to minimize the distinctions and mitigate the sense of alienation of these two closely related populations.

Under the iron rule of Tito, the newly founded state of Yugoslavia forged a union of groups that had existed in isolated hostility for generations. But as has been said by many, Tito was both the first and the last Yugoslav, and with his death the cultural hostilities that lay dormant emerged in bloody assaults on the traditional "enemies." These hatreds are symptoms based on nothing in the real world, but on something in the internal world of identities and enemies.

Can anyone pretend to distinguish the Irish Protestant from his Catholic equivalent in physical appearance, speech patterns, Irish traits, Celtic humor, or even cultural values? Only when the discussion turns to religious politics do the enmity and the differences emerge. In an Irish-American bar, no one has any idea whether the Callahan or Kelly with whom one is speaking is Catholic or Protestant. The same is true for the traveler in

Northern Ireland. A person's roots become apparent only when the discussion turns political. Then the degree of hatred that can emerge is nothing short of astonishing. These hatreds were sucked into the unconscious of the younger generations along with the wholesale adoption of the personae of the elders through the processes of identification. A channel for "inherited" hatred was created between parent and child.

The identification that I have just briefly discussed I have labeled "upward identification." That is not necessarily the most elegant term, but it is one that serves to contrast it with another and somewhat different form of identification called, naturally, "downward identification," with which I will compare it. Downward identification is another thing entirely from the identification of the child with the parent.

What is one to make of the almost instant identification that the parent makes with the child at the moment of its birth? The experience I underwent on seeing my own children for the first time was an epiphany. It seemed more closely related to things I had read about than other experiences I could recall. It appeared much more akin to that instant bonding of a duckling for the first object it perceives moving than to traditional human modes of relating. Unlike friendship, which takes time to evolve; unlike love, which requires sharing, vulnerability, trust, and commitment—this had the quality of a mechanical or chemical reaction.

Why even call it identification? It does not have the trappings of the traditional identifications practiced by the child growing up. We don't model ourselves after our children. We may adopt some of their interests, and we ought to be able to be influenced by their sensibilities. But we don't go through anything like the wholesale adoption of mannerisms, tastes, judgments, or values that is a part of the process of growing up. What relates the two forms of identification—upward and downward—is something called fusion.

The basic ingredient that defines identification is not the un-conscious modeling, but the fusion of the stuff of our very self with the substance of another. Identity starts by knowing the toe we bite is a part of us, and the teething ring or a maternal nipple is something other. With fusion there is an erosion of the rigid boundaries of self, a blurring of the sense of the isolated "I," or ego.

With upward identification, the child mentally "injests" the image of the parent and then fuses his own sense of self with that now-internalized image of his parent. The parental figure be-comes a part of the self. So much a part, that the child, willy-nilly, takes over many of the attitudes and actions of the parent in an unthinking and wholesale manner. This "fusion" of the two identities is what is referred to as identification. Identification blurs the distinction between the perceived self and the incorpo-rated person. It is nonetheless a selective process—there are mul-tiple models we take in. And it is a gradual process, one of which the child is almost totally unaware.

With the downward identification that a parent feels on first seeing her newborn child, the process of fusion tends to be total, instantaneous, and wonderfully conscious. If anything, the con-fusion about where we end and the child begins is more pro-found in this direction than the other. With the identification of love, a union occurs that binds one's fate to another's. To praise my child offers me praise. To do damage to my child is to injure me and will cause me greater pain than to harm me directly. It may be the greatest pain. The grief over the loss of a child is the open, festering, and agonizing sore of Philoctetes—the wound that never heals.

For some reason, the response to my first grandchild is now more vivid in my memory than the birth of my own children. I had seen this child within an hour of his birth and with that see-ing knew, not just understood, the meaning of biological imprinting. His image seemed to course through me like some secret message to an internal computer readjusting all the patterns of my consciousness. To the lifetime of experiences that had shaped my characteristic perceptions and behavior, a new experience had been added of such magnitude that a new sensibility, a changed me, was created. I knew that from that time on, that image was unshakably within me—an essential part of me—and, in some way that I did not yet understand, would inevitably alter, in ways that I could not predict, all my awareness and all my judgments.

What exactly happens in this identification with a child? I did not "swallow up," introject, this grandchild, or my two daughters before him. I have done the opposite. I had somehow or other catapulted myself into their shells. I have inserted "me" into them. My children are containers, and fragile ones at that, which cradle, not just my hopes and my ambitions, my aspirations and my vanities, but my essential self. They are me. With this kind of identification, we have located our core within another corpus. We have placed our destiny in a body under someone else's control. If my child does something foolhardy or willfully self-destructive, the pain will be experienced by hapless and innocent me. In great part this explains why no one is as capable of enraging us as our own children. They carry the helpless parent within them during all their reckless escapades. How dare she risk the purpose of my existence, my only immortality, my existential "meaning," and the person I most cherish, by endangering herself? This explains the evident distress and horror of the mother of the suicide bomber, even as she is claiming pride for his action.

Downward identification has the power and tenacity that one associates with the fixed instincts of animals—biologically driven and species-preserving devices. Unfortunately, in this area too, downward identification can be modified and abandoned through the capacities of the human beings to change their very natures. Fortunately, it generally operates almost universally like a "maternal instinct." It brings into play all the protective devices in a human mother to preserve her child, and thus the species. One can observe the same kind of behavior in the protective maneuvers of a doe. By protecting her offspring, the mother, animal or human, carries genes forward beyond the limited span of her lifetime. Her child will transport essential components of her self to her own children and the future generations.

These processes of identification are central in comprehending the limits of empathy and the contradictions of the workings of conscience. They help us understand our exquisite sensitivity to the pain of some and our indifference to—even our pleasure in—the pain of some others.

To complete an understanding of the mechanisms of empathy or indifference, I must introduce another principle of identification, particularly relevant to group identifications. I call this "proximal identification." Proximal identification is not a moral principle but a psychological reality, an indisputable, universal phenomenon. It is best understood by comparing our varying responses to tragic events.

There is no question that an injury to my child, even of a relatively trivial sort, hurts me more than a more serious injury to the child of a stranger. In my sensibilities my child's pain has a transcendent priority over your child's pain. I am not pleased or proud of this observation—it represents a limit on my capacity for empathy—but I am convinced it is true for you as well as for me. When I extend the argument even further, it becomes more appalling, but no less true. A severe trauma to my child, a scarring that would affect her life throughout her existence, would cause me more grief than the deaths of hundreds of thousands of children in the Sudan.

Let me clarify what I am saying. Of course I am distressed by the agony and injustices that have occurred in modern-day Africa, the starving in Somalia, the butchery and enslavement in the Sudan, the kidnapping and maiming of thousands of children in Sierra Leone, the slaughter of innocents in Rwanda and Burundi. When I witness these tragedies on the faces of real people through the pictures on television, or in my imagination while I am reading the newspaper accounts, a true sense of grief overcomes me. It is not simply an intellectual response. But this grief has a pathetically ephemeral existence. Although I may maintain my intellectual involvement and moral commitment through political and relief activities, my true and enduring emotions will not be the same as the pain caused by my everyday awareness of the injured child with whom I share my life. The most refined of consciences, the most overdeveloped capacity for guilt, will nonetheless rebuke our logical sense of justice and override our sense of proportionality when we deal with the suffering of those we know and love—our own—in comparison with the suffering of some distant others.

We are grieved by the everyday, by what we see, and what is close. The priority of the news media in focusing on local over international news is a testament to the interests of their audiences. More true grief and tears are generated by the discovery of the body of a murdered child in the neighborhood than of hundreds of children killed in floods in Bangladesh. The nearby disaster has more meaning, even though lesser than the distant one. It is not a new idea. Hume observed more than two hundred years ago, "Pity depends, in a great measure, on the contiguity and even sight of the object."* And certainly the capacity for television to bring disaster into our very homes has expanded the population of those with whom we can identify.

Although proximal identification may not require the physical

---

*David Hume, *A Treatise of Human Nature,* ed. David Fate Norton and Mary J. Norton, Oxford Philosophical Texts (London: Oxford University Press, 2000), p. 239.

proximity to or sight of the individual that Hume suggested, it certainly requires something comparable, a clearly defined kinship, for example. Such kinship may allow us to identify with people we have never known. We can identify with those in a future too far for us to envision and back to a past we never experienced. The chaotic and random killings in Northern Ireland, taking the lives of hundreds of innocents, inevitably touched the hearts of Irish Americans who had never been in Ireland more than the loss of a hundred thousand lives in Iran. A terrorist bomb exploded in a bus full of Israeli children feels like a personal blow to an American Jew who has never been to Israel.

These ethnic and religious identifications—with the limitation of empathy they suggest—can be seen as deriving from important survival patterns built into our genetic matrix before the emergence of modern culture. Proximal identification may seem irrational and unjust in our current period, when we are approaching a global culture, but it was a biological necessity at an earlier period. Without it we could not have saved the species in those days of limited awareness of space and even more limited vision of the world as a whole. We preserved the species by each protecting his own. The units of survival in prehistoric times were much smaller than those of today. There were no nations, and there was no consideration of the universality of mankind. There were only family clusters, no "family of man." Survival of the species, particularly through the protection of the vulnerable young on whom the future rests, demands an overvaluation of the needs of those young who are our own specific charges.

We can see that among herding animals, the herd is best protected when the antelope protects her offspring, and hers alone, from the marauding lion. If every mother were concerned about all the young—the general welfare—none would survive. The propensity of human beings to overvalue their own is part of the biological inheritance we share with lower communal animals.

Having dealt professionally with human suffering on the most intimate level in my work with patients, I know that true empathy, producing real compassion and personal suffering, remains a proximal quality. Those rare individuals who have hearts that bleed indiscriminately for humanity in general are likely to have eyes that shed few tears for individual men and women.

The greatest protection against group hatred is the ultimate inclusion of the hated contingent into the population with which we identify. In other words, expand "proximal" identification to larger and larger constituencies. Part of the tragedy of the African states is that statehood was established arbitrarily under European colonialism. As such, the "states" were never identifiable or recognizable by the natives who were its presumed members. The result was that identities were fixed to relatively small units. When there was unification, it was through religion, which, as will later be discussed, managed not only to enlarge the community of identifying people but also to define a larger enemy population.

While not denying the existence of subcultures in the United States, with their multiple divisions into "us" and "them" and the consequent prejudices, what is still amazing is that we have managed to forge a national identity among widely diverse populations. We do have an *American* identity, and when an American naval ship, the USS *Cole*, was attacked by terrorists, we responded in unity with appropriate grief and anger, independent of whether the victims were black or white, Christian or Jew, northern or southern, rich or poor.

We have made progress. Aided by the shrinking world of modern travel and the instant awareness made possible through modern communications, we are approaching a global community. We have gone from family to clan to nation. A nation of almost three hundred million grieved over the bombing of the World Trade Center in New York. To a lesser extent, a community of similar cultures shared our grief. We can hope for a time when we approach that broadest of identifications, but we must be realistic. The "family of man" is a noble ideal that will never be realized. Nevertheless, noble and impossible ideals serve useful purposes. Few Christians can embrace and live the life of Christ, but in aspiring to do so they may become better people.

Proximal identification can never be extended to include the entire human race. Its biological purpose is exactly the opposite. We serve the species by overvaluing that small section of it for which we are responsible. Yearning for a true "brotherhood of man" is hopeless. There is no psychological way to extend our downward identification to all. It is too heavy a burden. Were each of us to grieve over the suffering of every child in the same way as we do with our own, life would be unendurable. Just as the surgeon must protect himself from the suffering of his patients to facilitate his professional role, we cannot mourn in the truest sense over every tragedy in the daily paper. We are touched and empathic, and that is the most we can expect. That is also the least we should expect of ourselves. We cannot tolerate total indifference.

But what if, beyond indifference, we take delight? We have then moved from the relative indifference that we maintain toward the other and into the area of hatred that we reserve for our enemies. Hatred is an extreme and perverse distortion of the necessary process of group identification. The entire process of identity and identification involves not just locating ourselves but also locating others. It is a method of separation as well as identification. If there is a "me," then there is a "not-me," which will eventually be further identified as things and other people. If there exists a group of people with whom I identify and with whom I share a common fate, there must be others with whom I do not identify.

To say that I do not identify with some group is still short of wishing its members ill. It may simply mean that I have no emotional investment in them, no primary concern for them, and little empathy for them. It is a form of prejudice to exclude a whole population from our moral sensibilities, but it is well short of hatred. When I said that the opposite of both love and hate is indifference, it is to this lack of identification that I referred.

This exclusion from identity explains the relative indifference that exists in the more developed countries to the suffering in the less developed world. Even the compassionate vocation of medicine has neglected the search for treatments for crippling diseases that are endemic to alien environments. Schistosomiasis and filariasis, parasitic diseases of the tropics, commanded relatively little research, considering the tragic suffering they cause, when compared with the search for the cures for common allergies. It is not just that there is less money to be made—although that is the primary driver of pharmacological research—but that in general these areas are simply less visible to most of us. We don't hate these people. They just don't command our attention.

Certainly there is a bias here. The people affected do not have a strong moral claim on us. They are not members of our community. And while I am hopeful that we can eventually become more inclusive and expand the community of the us, I am well aware that the nature of proximal identification will always place people on a continuum of closeness to our hearts. Still, such indifference begins the process that makes the other not just different from, but less than, us. Indifference and bias are dangerous because they are natural way stations on the road to enmity. Locating an alien other encourages and unleashes the forces of hatred that lie dormant in the biased individual.

11

IDENTIFYING
THE ENEMY

Indifference in the face of evil is in itself a moral wrong, but it is still not the active engagement that defines hatred. We must perceive the other as a danger, an enemy, in order to begin to hate him. But more important, we must have an internal conflict for which the location of an enemy will supply some resolution and relief. A sense of personal worthlessness, helplessness, and despair characterize a diminished and desperate individual. Such a population is the soil in which the seeds of hatred may be sown.

There have been beaten down and deprived populations that have passively endured without hatred for centuries. Their condition was accepted by them as an existential fact of life, not a humiliation imposed from above. Indeed, when supported by religion, the impoverished life may be viewed as a key to the kingdom of heaven. "And again I say unto you, It is easier for a camel to go through the eye of a needle, than for a rich man to enter into the kingdom of God."*

Only when we feel that we have actively been deprived—or sense that we have been denied that to which we are entitled—will we seek some external cause of our adversity. When the cause is perceived as within our nature, our own fault, we despair; if the cause is perceived as imposed from outside, we are ripe for hatred. The change from despair to feeling humiliated and exploited involves shifting responsibility from the self to others. It requires identifying an enemy. When the other is indeed the oppressor, a revolutionary rage (a righteous anger) may be liberated. But more often that not, a scapegoat population is targeted, one that bears no responsibility for the perceived or real injuries. This scapegoating is the paranoid mechanism behind hatred. It is why most group hatred may be viewed as an irrational phenomenon.

The choice of the enemy will not be totally arbitrary, even when it is at heart an irrational choice. It must *seem* rational to the hater, which is the basis of rationalization. The choice may be territorial—bearing some historic rationalization for the current hatred—or the enemy may be selected on ideological grounds. In either case, it is my thesis that the choice will always be in the service of scapegoating.

Scapegoating

Jean-Paul Sartre, in his brilliant (but deeply flawed) essay, *Anti-Semite and Jew,* made two profound observations.† He indicated:

---

*Matthew 19:24.

†Sartre, still in the throes of Marxism, wrote: "We find scarcely any anti-Semitism among workers. . . . The majority of the anti-Semites . . . belongs to

"Anti-Semitism . . . is something quite other than an idea. It is . . . a passion."* And later, the much-quoted statement: "Far from experience producing his [the anti-Semite's] idea of the Jew, it was the latter which explained his experience. If the Jew did not exist, the anti-Semite would invent him."† These two statements expand the concept of hatred beyond a mere emotional experience and beyond the confines of reality.

An enemy is defined as a "foe": "One who feels hatred toward, intends injury to, or opposes the interests of another." Enmity, real enmity, exists between nations as between individuals. There are opposing personal and national interests that are perceived as threatening. I use the word "perceived" because with the perspective of hindsight, many conflicts—in both the individual and the national arena—that were fought on the assumption of real injury or threat proved to be conflicts of ego. It is hard to discern the "real" principles defended in the monstrous slaughter of World War I. Still, there were and will be true enemies and legitimate conflicts, but those are a minority. For hate-driven groups such as the Nazis, Al Qaeda, or the Ku Klux Klan, the enemy is more often a convenience than a true threat. The enemy is a necessary device to alleviate a sense of shame, humiliation, and impotence. If no traditional enemy is at hand, one must be created.

The enemy becomes an essential ingredient in the life of the haters. Like a delusion, it is created to serve the needs of the hater. And also like the typical symptom, it invariably represents a displacement of a conflict from the internal world of the person

---

the middle class, that is, among men who have a level of life equal or superior to that of the Jews." Jean-Paul Sartre, *Anti-Semite and Jew*, tran. George J. Becker (New York: Schocken, 1965), pp. 35–36.

*Ibid., p. 10.

†Ibid., p. 13.

to an outside agency. We alleviate our internal conflicts and protect our self-esteem by placing the source of our misery outside of our own area of culpability; we find some other to blame. After having found that other, we can absolve ourselves of responsibility; view our inadequacies as products of external assault; and vent our spleen on the enemy, taking comfort in "fighting back" rather than suffering the humiliation of passive acceptance. An enemy adds purpose, passion, and hope to a dismal existence. The enemy must be found, and if one is not readily available in the political or social world around us, an enemy must be created out of whole cloth. The true purpose of an enemy will be to serve the modus vivendi, the lifestyle, of the hater. Understanding hatred requires treating it as a metaphor and searching for the symbolic displacements.

The classic and most direct example of displacement occurs in Leviticus with the story of the sacrificial goat, the literal scapegoat.

> And Aaron shall lay both his hands upon the head of the live
> goat, and confess over him all iniquities of the children of Israel,
> and all their transgressions, even all their sins; and he shall put
> them upon the head of the goat, and shall send him away by the
> hand of an appointed man into the wilderness. And the goat shall
> bear upon him all their iniquities unto a land which is cut off.*

In the biblical text, the story of the scapegoat depicts a symbolic gesture, a metaphor to show God's mercy and forgiveness. The displacement is conscious and its meaning apparent to the participants. The goat was, along with bullocks and rams, a traditional sacrificial animal and seems arbitrarily selected. When Shirley Jackson wrote "The Lottery," a modern fable of scapegoating, substituting a human member of the community for the

---

*Leviticus 16:22–23.

goat, the story became an instant classic of terror.* This simple tale, told in everyday language, exploited an element of human nature as a vehicle for horror: We do not want to know that we are prepared to sacrifice the innocent for our own purposes. When we commit moral crimes for selfish reasons, we want to pretend that we commit these wrongs in the service of the good. We deny we are attending anything so trivial as our ego, but claim we are serving God and country.

Scapegoating, as used today, is an attempt to place our own transgression onto the shoulders of a target group. The purpose is no longer to seek God's forgiveness in penitence and honesty but rather to avoid guilt by denying responsibility. Therefore, the displacement is unconscious—otherwise it would be simple deceit—its purposes disguised from both victim and victimizer. And the sacrificial group is rarely arbitrarily selected. To maintain the self-deception, the selection must be sufficiently artful in design to seem credible. The displacement must be of such a nature that it seems to make sense. The scapegoated group will, however, always carry some symbolic clue as to the nature of the internal conflicts that they are symbolically being used to resolve.

The severity of the anxiety that tortures a psychotic individual demanding respite is such that the rationalization that will be used to explain it must be of a proportionate dimension. A patient must fabricate a monstrous evil. If the person turns to hypochondria to rationalize his anxiety, the disease he selects must be equal to his terror. It will not do to perceive his imaginary illness as chicken pox or conjunctivitis. In order to rationalize severe

---

*Shirley Jackson, "The Lottery," *New Yorker*, June 28, 1948. That was the same year in which Sartre published his essay *Anti-Semite and Jew*. During the immediate postwar period, with the beginning awareness of the extent of the Holocaust and the passive complicity that accompanied it, a literature of self-examination emerged.

anxiety, he will perceive symptoms of cancer or heart failure. Similarly, with the classic paranoid delusion, the forces opposing the individual must also be perceived as formidable and life threatening. They must be aliens of great cunning, the devil or his agents. In destroying the enemy, the paranoid wants to feel he is saving not just himself, but his country or, as with Schreber, redeeming the entire race of man. The individual will be supported—more often, directed—by an equally powerful ally. He will view himself as the agent of the president of the United States or of God himself.

Those who are not delusional do not have the capacity to distort or ignore reality sufficiently to claim that the devil or aliens from Mars are out to destroy them. Instead, they must locate their enemies in the real world among their traditional antagonists. Not all of these antagonists will at first be perceived with a deeply ingrained hatred. That will emerge in time. The object of group hatred is often a product of calculated propaganda generated to mobilize the population. During a period of actual conflict, as in wartime, a concerted campaign must be launched to demonize the enemy. This propaganda will facilitate the assaults on morality that are inevitable in wartime. Often these wartime hatreds disappear faster than they are created. To the shock of most Americans, within a period of time no longer than the conflict itself, the German and Japanese enemies became our allies in the Cold War against our former ally and new enemy, the Russians.

We are free to locate enemies anywhere, but it is always easier to place blame on a traditional enemy, to revive past grievances, and by so doing, to rationalize our choice. When locating enemies, therefore, we are likely to start by looking at our neighbors. I have labeled such enemies as "territorial." At the opposite end of the spectrum are enemies whom we could not recognize on contact, but whose ideologies offend us, and who may be labeled "ideological enemies." These terms—territorial and ideological—

are part of a seamless whole, since even those based on actual territorial disputes inevitably will require an ideological component to perpetuate a lasting hatred.

Ideological enemies may be built on a framework of true ideological differences, such as in religious wars. But as with the Christian Crusades, there is often a crude territorial objective hidden within these "ideological" struggles. Sometimes enemies seem to be manufactured out of chance and coincidence. The Holocaust was constructed out of the paranoid needs of the German leaders, since the Jews in Germany were a tiny minority and were by most objective standards simply "Germans" in their day-to-day behavior and their loyalty to the Fatherland.

It is often only too obvious that the "enemy" is merely a convenient contrivance to serve some inner anguish and rage. This is particularly apparent in the often drunken "let's get them" Saturday night entertainments that once were endemic throughout America and that involved tormenting blacks, Jews, gays, or whatever despised group could be found. What is more difficult to perceive is that even when there are true ideological differences, the ideology itself is rarely the issue. Here, too, the primary purpose is to find a rational alternative to ourselves and our leaders as the source of our deprivations and misery and as an outlet for our anger. The goal is to shift the blame.

The Territorial Enemy: The Enemy at Hand

The injunction "to love thy neighbor as thyself" has always seemed to me to be the most unreasonable directive in the New Testament. This casual statement in Leviticus was embraced and elevated in importance in the New Testament, where love rather than justice played the central role. The Old Testament is a practical guide for living, and its Ten Commandments are a possible, though admittedly difficult, code of conduct to maintain. The commandments also attend to our behavior with our neighbors. They proscribe both "coveting" and "bearing false witness against" one's neighbors. But *loving* your enemy as you love yourself or your loved ones? This seems to me beyond the reach of most human beings. One is more likely to "love" a stranger or an abstraction—humankind—than the competitor at the borders of your private space. I have made the point that identity is proximal. Love and hate both are founded in the cauldron of identity. One is more likely to hate one's neighbor than a distant creature who does not impinge on or limit one's actions. The injunction to love thy neighbor as thyself is deemed so central to the Christian ideal that this same directive appears at least five times in the New Testament.* But then, Christianity is a religion that motivates its followers by an image of admittedly unattainable perfection. The New Testament simply wants you to try and allows for forgiveness

These cautionary statements about one's neighbor—not rules of general decorum among people—implicitly recognize that the most likely source of war and conflict in earlier history would involve those others who are at our borders. It specifically pinpoints the competitive rivalries in early times, when communities were small, competition for food and water great, and mutual cooperation for a larger good not yet anticipated. The injunction to love thy neighbor serves a political as well as an ethical purpose. At the least, it was a prophylactic attempt to inhibit the emergence of hatred in neighboring communities by aspiring to brotherly love.

The history of civilization is a matter of a paltry few thousand years in the millions of years that our species, Homo sapiens, has existed. By definition, we have no records or proofs of the exact

---

*See Matthew, Mark, Romans, Galatians, and James.

nature of prehistoric life. We have some knowledge. We can roughly date the discovery of metals, tools, and agricultural techniques. We have cave drawings that date and define hunting procedures. What we do not have is any evidence, any record, of what the prehistoric people *thought*.

While we cannot know the content of their ideas, we do know that the minds of our ancestors must have operated according to the same principles as ours. After all, in anthropological terms, they are separated from us by only moments of time. Being of the same species, they share the same physiology and potential. No mutations or genetic changes could have possibly been established during such a minimal time frame. We differ from our late prehistoric ancestors only culturally, in the way that the Bedouins of North Africa differ from New Yorkers.

Early people clustered together for the group survival demanded by our biology. They operated under the same genetic systems governing the same biological imperatives that influence us today. We can safely assume that they protected the helpless child, shared the tasks of providing food, clothing, and shelter for the community essential to the social animal that we are. They established group identities, group beliefs, group totems, and religions. They defined an "us" and thus, by definition again, an "other." The groups, however, were small and the enemy was at hand.

Early enemies resided on the other side of the hill or mountain range in areas staked out by each group as its preserve, if not yet its nation. What was preserved were matters of life and death—hunting areas or grazing grounds. When the enemy raided your territory, he took with him the stuff of your group survival and, in the process, killed your people and raped your women. It would not be long before the very existence of the other would be perceived as a threat to survival. We hated the person who threatened the life of our loved ones, who murdered our children. Since travel was limited—picture life on a small island—the enemy was the same enemy that persisted for generations, and a true obsession was inevitable.

The hatred felt then and the suffering it caused were the same as that which we feel today toward those who threaten us and those we love. But in one sense, hatred seems to have been more justifiable, more rational in the days of the tribal strife. In those smaller environments where food had to be gathered almost daily, life was lived in a tenuous present and a zero-sum game for survival existed. Their feast and our famine were intricately linked. The very existence of the neighboring tribe, not just their isolated actions of cruelty, was a threat to the lives of our children.

The conflicts between neighbors that exist today are almost invariably more symbol than substance. Nevertheless, territory, whether the vast territory of Kashmir or the small Shaba'a farmlands area that define the border between Israel and Lebanon, is used as a focus of enmity. Territory is particularly pertinent in that it demonstrates how land may be used as a rationalization and validating reason for sustaining hatred.

Territory has enormous emotional leverage in the minds of most individuals. It is concrete, can be visualized, and perpetuates the idea of desecrated "homeland." Territory gives tangible focus to grievances that are rooted in altogether different dynamics. It helps define the enemy.

The Irish Protestant and the Irish Catholic are separated, defined really, by their religion, but it is territory that they fight over. If one could solve the political status of Northern Ireland in a way that seems to provide respect for each party and pays tribute to the real or imagined grievances of the past, one suspects that the religious differences would prove to be readily accommodated. The land has become the metaphor for that emotional condition called "national pride." If our country is strong, somehow we must be stronger than the evidence of our daily life suggests. To a creature that lives in the world of its own perception, the symbol transcends actuality in importance. Human beings respond to the metaphor, for good and bad.

Think of the national jubilation verging on hysteria that seems the inevitable response to a country's winning the World Cup in soccer. Our team—composed of disadvantaged people like us—has vanquished, indeed humiliated, the mighty. Never mind that it is only a game, and the moment that it is over, we must resume our impoverished lives. On the field of games and through the imaginative power of group identification, *we* have triumphed. An economically struggling country goes wild over winning a soccer match, as though it were the discovery of vast reserves of oil, and in the process actually feels more joy and pride. The World Cup places them at the top of the heap, if only symbolically and if only for moments.

Everywhere in the modern world where traditional enmities exist—Ireland, the Middle East, Kashmir, the Sudan—there is a division into self and others that focuses on territory. And everywhere the territory will turn out to be a symbol.

The Burundi-Rwanda wars are particularly devastating examples of long-term battles over largely symbolic territory. The massacres between Hutu and Tutsi occurred time and again over decades, resulting in the slaughter of hundreds of thousands. It is hard to identify a starting point for the conflict. The intermingling of these people extends back at least a half century, but beyond that little can be verified.* Popular knowledge has it that Tutsi cattle herders migrated south from their homes in Ethiopia into the Great Lakes area then occupied by the Hutus. This migration set the stage for a primary claim to the area by the Hutus,

---

*The attention of the American and European press was not captured until the relatively recent Hutu-Tutsi massacres that erupted after Rwanda's President Habyrimana's plane was shot down by a surface-to-air missile in 1994.

reminiscent of some of the rhetoric in the Israeli-Palestinian conflicts, as to who "got there first." Current scholarship indicates that there is no proof that the Hutus' claim is true. Revisionist histories exist on both sides, yet what is clear is that a conflict between the Hutu and the Tutsi has existed over hundreds of years—preceding colonization, although undoubtedly exacerbated by it. The conditions of the recurring massacres and the rationalizations for them would change with each episode of destruction. But a traditional rivalry over land existed and serves as a classic example of tribalism at its worst.

With the Hutu-Tutsi conflicts, the occupations of common grounds and the slaughter increased and the pace of enslavement of the enemy accelerated with each shift of the power struggle. The withdrawal of the Belgians in 1959 saw constant battles to fill the power vacuum, resulting in the splitting of the area into two states. In this case the split into two separate and arbitrary countries in Africa was no more effective in ameliorating hostilities than the opposite was in Europe—the joining of separate Balkan states into the arbitrary single country of Yugoslavia. Neither political maneuver seemed to help dispel traditional and established enmities. Eventually the same conflicts would emerge in both Rwanda and Burundi as had existed in the conjoint state. Only the identity of the victims and victimizers changed, depending on the shifts of power. The battleground was the same.

The Ideological Enemy

Since hatred is inevitably a displacement, the hater generally needs a known population on which to displace his or her resentment. The Hutus needed proximity to create an enemy population. They were not likely to select as an enemy the Inuits of the Arctic Circle, of whose presence they were not even aware. They also needed a history of grievances. Territorial conflicts are a substantial ingredient in sustaining old enmities. The presence of the enemy, his physical approximation—the "vision" of him, as Hume would have it—plays a central role in hatred, as it does in pity and compassion.

Enemies are generally drawn from the neighborhood and ordinarily derived from a long tradition of contact and conflict. In most of the sustaining enmities, although proximity was a necessary condition for locating an enemy, one still needed some identifying differences—some potential threat. National differences will do. But short of some history of atrocities between the two populations, national differences create identities too weak to sustain hatred over time.

Think of the peculiar modern history between two other groups of people, the Americans and the Vietnamese. The corrosive hatred between the Americans and the Viet Cong during the war was staggering. To the North Vietnamese, the American intruders were heirs to the French occupiers, yet another wave of colonizing Caucasians intruding on their space and destroying their population in the process. To the Americans the North Vietnamese were a Communist menace, the first of the dominoes, and another "yellow peril" for a society still struggling with vestigial racism. Some three million Vietnamese died in that war. And it permanently altered the relationship of millions of Americans to their government.

The peace agreement between the Americans and the Vietnamese was signed on January 27, 1973. Now, thirty years later, what can we make of the relationship that exists between these two enemies so recently engaged in deadly struggle? Vietnamese now join the other immigrants from Asia to the United States, greeted with the same ambiguity, but no more hostility, than the Japanese, Koreans, and Chinese that preceded them. Americans, bored with the more familiar cuisines of China, Japan, and Thailand, are now making Vietnamese cooking the latest rage. For the most part, Americans do not think of the Vietnamese. And in Vietnam? Well, if we are to believe David Lamb—a former war correspondent living in peacetime Hanoi—they positively love Americans:

> When Fidel Castro visited Hanoi . . . officials had to bus kids in from the countryside and give them Cuban flags to make a crowd. Russian President Vladimir Putin attracted nothing more than yawns and a score or so of curious onlookers outside his hotel. . . . But for Clinton, the Vietnamese went nuts! . . . Vietnamese by the tens of thousands stood six-deep along the airport road. . . . Another huge crowd gathered outside the Daewoo Hotel to cheer his arrival. . . . Everywhere Clinton went for three days there were multitudes of cheering young people.*

There is, in other words, no residual hatred and no sign of an attachment in enmity. Quite the contrary, today Vietnam looks to America as a model of a successful economy to which it aspires. And Americans, in typical fashion, have pretty much dismissed Vietnam from their minds. Vietnam now takes its position among the vast hordes of countries whose existence has no current significance for the people of the United States. It is relegated to the area of apathy and indifference that one reserves for those who have no role to play in our emotional life.

There was never a territorial relationship between Vietnam and the United States. And the ideological relationship that was falsely presumed to be present died with the end of the Cold War. The Vietnamese, having won the war, emerged with their pride enhanced. They were not the humiliated party. There is no sense

---

*David Lamb, *Vietnam, Now: A Reporter Returns* (New York: Public Affairs, 2002), p. 264.

of national despair. Instead, the rage of the past is obscured by a continuing struggle to rebuild and enhance the economy. Vietnam has essentially abandoned the Communist model. Having been proved a failure in every country that had the misfortune to adopt it, communism exists in modern Vietnam only in the remnants of political nomenclature. Capitalism is the new standard and the exemplar is that of the United States. There are, therefore, none of the traditional grounds for hatred remaining.

To sustain hatred, one cannot simply view the enemy as another set of people. The enemy must be evil and a menace to our well-being. Some means must be established to justify violation of normal codes of behavior when dealing with the enemy. To this purpose, the enemy will be demonized, made into an agent of evil, or, worse, dehumanized so that the rules that apply to conduct among people can be suspended.

Wartime requires a rapid demonizing of the enemy in order to justify the kind of injury that one must inflict on enemy populations, inevitably including the innocent among them. But as seen in the relationship between the Americans and Vietnamese, the bonds of hatred can melt quickly with a very short thaw. Similarly the hated Boche of World War I seemed to disappear with the romanticizing of Germany and German culture in the 1920s and early 1930s. Berlin would become a Bohemian capital for English and American writers.

Sustained hatreds are created when "ideological" differences, specifically religious ones, remain festering, long after political settlements are agreed upon. The dissolution of Yugoslavia into multiple groups of hatred is a prime example. The Serbs attribute their hatred of the Muslims to a humiliation dating back to the invasion of Kosovo Polje in 1389. Their hatred for the Croats antedated even this by centuries.

As the history of Yugoslavia demonstrates, in many cases the confluence between territory and ideology makes any exact differentiation arbitrary. Often, an ideological difference will simply serve to fulfill material desires. One would have to be a sophisticated theologian to detect any life-threatening or otherwise profound differences between the Roman Catholic and Greek Orthodox theologies. History had imposed a different identity on these ethnically similar Slavs. Religious identity, not ethnicity, sustained the Slavs' sense of enmity over the centuries. Religious differences became fused with differing political ideologies in the Balkans. The recent Serbian slaughter of the Bosnian Muslims was entirely territorial. The ideologies helped to demonize the Muslims and justify the genocidal slaughter that followed. The ideologies masked a pure grab for territory.

Ideological enemies can best be examined when no territory or national interest is present to obfuscate the issues—when the politics are removed and the passion is focused. In this case it is easier to turn to such groups as the antiabortion fanatics, the radical animal rights activists, and the extreme environmental-protection movements, groups that bomb and kill in the service of some ideological principle that transcends all others. They have subordinated all other moral commitments to their one moral crusade.

In my research for this book, I visited many of the websites of radical reformist groups in an attempt to understand the motivation and means for forming ideological communities. I started with simple causes, usually single-issue groups. Specifically, I wanted to understand how groups that had been formed ostensibly out of compassion, to protect the helpless and abused—animals, children, nature—were so readily converted to a community of haters. How love of the victim became subordinate to hatred of those who do not share one's belief.

Most right-to-lifers, animal rights people, environmental protection groups, while passionately devoted to their causes, would not commit acts of violence or condone such actions by others.

Still, in their "righteous" indignation against the opponents, they set a climate of hatred and create a defined and legitimate community in which the paranoid can enlist. These groups offer the individual hater an outlet for his groundless hatred, a self-justifying rationalization for his frustration, and a group identity that generally eludes the isolated and mistrusting paranoid.

The websites are, I suspect, the domain of the fringe elements of movements, representing a radical minority. It is their personal agendas that preempt the true goals of their cause. In addition, these sites provide justification for the even sicker segment of their constituency—those who are actually prepared to do violence. These people, who are at the periphery of the movement, are not primarily motivated by the specific cause—say, their anxiety for despoilation of the earth—but rather by their need to find relief from perceived persecutions and humiliations. The rhetoric supplied them by the leadership has both a religious fervor and the absolute certitude of revealed truth. This messianic leadership supplies those struggling with personal demons a rational and noble reason to destroy innocent life, at the same time, relieving their internal conflicts.

These websites have become a nucleus for the formation of a community of haters. They are a haven for such paranoid psychotics as Theodore Kaczynski. The movement supplies a rationalizing factor that supports the psychotic's delusional thinking. The rage he feels and the destruction he exercises are now justified as being in the service of some common good. What he is doing may seem evil but is actually "noble" and "proper," "a service to morality." This justification is confirmed by his allegiances.

Ted Kaczynski stated in court that he used information from the "Litha 1993" *Earth First Journal* to kill Thomas Mosser by sending a bomb to his home. His conviction that he was saving the entire world was sufficient justification for him to say in a letter to the *New York Times*, dated June 24, 1995, "We have no regret about the fact that our bomb blew up the wrong man, Gilbert Murray, instead of William Dennison, to whom it was addressed."

Radical single-issue groups offer justification for personal paranoia by the extreme rhetoric of their publications. But a mass culture of hatred cannot possibly be composed entirely, or preponderantly, of madmen and psychopaths. These websites are capable of attracting and mobilizing hatred, but they are likely to draw into their webs only people previously disposed to hatred.

The antiabortion activists see abortion as infanticide. In their battle to save the innocent, the taking of a few less-innocent lives—doctors and nurses and parents ready to "kill" their own babies—seems to them a reasonable moral trade-off. In their perverse utilitarian thinking, they will have saved more lives than they have taken. Their current campaigns on the web employ the term "the abortion holocaust," by which they choose to see direct equivalence between abortion and the Holocaust. They argue that while the Holocaust killed 6,000,000 Jews, since *Roe v. Wade* (1973), "28,000,000 unborn babies have been put to death by abortion in this country."* They believe they are fighting the just war, and under that aegis, the use of an atomic weapon to further their cause may be justified. They are free to kill the few to save the many. Incidentally, the Catholic church and the fundamentalist Protestant churches, whose philosophies underlie the right-to-life action groups, were not nearly so outspoken during the Holocaust. The passivity of Christian communities in the face of the Holocaust slaughter continues to be exposed in current studies and stands in sharp contrast to the passion with which they currently defend against abortion and even birth control.

Abortion—The Hidden Holocaust. abortionfacts.com/literature/literature-927hh.asp.

Many animal rights activists perceive helpless animals as akin to innocent babies. Thus the life of a laboratory mouse is fungible with the life of a laboratory technician. To prevent torture to the helpless, the activists are willing to bomb the facilities of the torturers—the research laboratories of major hospitals—and in the process risk the loss of some of the "torturers" or their "enablers." Equating human life with animal life, even if a ratio of value is applied, opens the door to the kind of utilitarian arguments that justify murder in the defense of animals.

The preservation of the environment is another focus for purely ideological enmity. Until fairly recently, environmental groups eschewed violence. Over the past few years, however, they have moved into active aggression. The Earth Liberation Front has so far specifically targeted only research facilities, offices, and equipment. But the rhetoric level has been rising, and eventually the groups justify the direct targeting of people. Their setting fire to the construction site for the Microbial and Plant Genomics Research Center at the University of Minnesota's St. Paul campus in January 2002 is frighteningly reminiscent of the actions of Ted Kaczynski. After the accidental death that occurred, the activists tried to justify the murder on utilitarian grounds, comparing it to the incidental deaths of civilians in a war zone. Once such a philosophical argument has been made, it stands as an a priori basis for any extreme member to extend the violence intentionally. This is the pattern that has evolved in the pro-life activist community as well.

Despite the occasional abuses of the fanatic fringe elements that accumulate around all protest groups, I would not classify the three ideological communities cited above as cultures of hatred. The vast majority of their memberships clearly are not violent. But all three of them have spawned satellite groups that are classic single-issue radicals, for whom the importance of their cause transcends, and worse, preempts other values and virtues.

In addition, these radicals are prepared to risk the death of others in their passionate pursuits. All three groups lend themselves to the crusader mentality and, wittingly or not, encourage terrorism by utilizing language that is incendiary and apocalyptic. And all three causes have already produced followers who have executed murderous assaults on innocent people. For these reasons, the leaders of these groups have some moral responsibility for the evil done in their name.

The ideological enemy is conceived as doing evil and, thus, lends an element of righteousness to our hatred; the territorial enemy offers a past reality, if not a present threat, which can be used to justify hatred. The scapegoat, on the other hand, is an enemy manufactured out of whole cloth. Most cultures of hatred combine all three elements in their scenarios of hatred. To the chagrin of devout and decent believers, the forces that have seemed best capable of fusing all the elements into a culture of hatred have been the orthodoxies represented by organized religions.

To summarize: To forge a hate-driven group like Al Qaeda, there must be present a dynamic internal *need* for an enemy. Then the enemy must be located. The enemy will not be chosen at random. Proximity is important, but not essential. Ideological differences also serve the purpose. The choice of the "enemy" will be dictated by fear, rage, guilt, or envy. With fear, guilt, and rage, some grievance, real or perceived, directs the hatred. With envy, the victim may have no presence in the life of the hater. The victim is purely a scapegoat. These dynamics are brought together most clearly in the context of a culture of hatred, which we must now examine.

THE CULTURES OF
HATRED

12

A CULTURE OF HATRED

There are two distinctly different types of communities dominated by hate. These communities are equally malevolent, but the difference in their structures point to differing means to prevent or confront them.

The first I have labeled a "culture of hatred"; the second, a "culture of haters." A culture of hatred is a natural community that breeds and encourages hatred. This is a group with a shared history and usually a shared locale, a country or its subculture. The leadership, the educational institutions, the dominant religious forces—individually or in concert—indoctrinate the members of the community with their venomous attitudes toward the designated enemy. Nazi Germany was a full-fledged culture of hatred. The Palestinians are an emerging one.

A culture of haters is an artificial community created when individuals who share a common hatred join forces in alliance against their enemy. They do not require a shared culture, history, language, or locality. The culture is an artificial one, formed of people with different backgrounds and disparate values. The members of these groups need not be indoctrinated. They come together only because of the shared enemy, with the hatred often being the only shared value. Al Qaeda and the various neo-Nazi movements across the world are examples of cultures of haters.

When considering the special qualities and natures that define different cultures, one is forced to make generalizations. That is dangerous, as one runs the risk of committing the same stereotyping that we condemn in bigotry. Yet in order to do justice to the profound influence cultures have on individuals, one must generalize.

We are not programmed insects. The way we are treated as we grow up will determine the nature of our character and, through that, our conduct. We cannot even determine whether a person is behaving irrationally or "normally" without considering the widely diverse demands of varying cultures. Our environment sets the values that define good and evil behavior. Thus, honorable and virtuous members of differing cultures will behave in ways that will be deemed shameful and immoral by contrasting cultures.

The Americans viewed the Japanese suicide bombers who were so effective and terrifying against the U.S. fleet at the end of World War II as madmen. The Japanese viewed these same suicide bombers as martyrs. Ritual suicide is a respectable tradition in Japan. In America suicide is almost invariably viewed as a sign of mental illness. So, although we Americans will honor the occasional soldier who throws himself on a grenade, we do not actually view this act as suicide, but rather a noble sacrifice of the treasured self to save the lives of comrades.

Americans have volunteered in every war for high-risk duties, but America could never have recruited a specific group of suicide bombers to hurl themselves at the enemy. Such volunteers would not have been at hand. More significant, the American public would never have understood or condoned their sacrifice. The waves of Americans who stormed the beaches in Normandy or hacked their way to the heights of Iwo Jima may have seemed to be involved in the same kind of suicidal assaults as the Japanese suicide bombers, but they were not. The intentions of the Japanese were to die in the service of their emperor, their country, and their religion. The Americans were prepared to die while hoping that they would survive. These contrary motivations reveal that the two seemingly similar activities are almost diametrically antithetical actions.

In making this comparison, I am not attributing a higher moral standing to one value over the other. Obviously, I have my values, but they have no relevance here. This analogy is not for the purposes of ascribing moral superiority or inferiority; I am not prepared here to call one behavior sick and the other healthy. The juxtaposition is presented to demonstrate that individual actions can be completely understood only within the culture from which they emerge. Nonetheless, I will make the case that some cultures are morally corrupt.

As a practicing psychiatrist, I am always aware of the specific culture in which a person is raised. Family values (in themselves influenced by culture) and the larger culture acting together shape the emerging conscience of the growing child. I obviously must attend to environmental influences in treating patients. When I do, I have to take into account the degree to which certain types of behavior are aberrant only by the standards of the society at large. Certain beliefs and conduct that are perfectly normal in one culture are signs of neurosis in another. This is equally true for subcultures in a diverse community like the United States. The psychiatrist who does not recognize these differences does a disservice to his patient. He may unfairly view something as neurotic that is perfectly normal in the subculture in which the patient was raised. Certainly a committed Mormon boy from a small town in Utah who practiced sexual abstinence until marriage should be viewed differently from the thirty-two-year-old virgin raised by bohemian parents in Greenwich Village. I respect the validity of such cultural differences. Like differences as to sexual conduct, subcultures nurture diverse attitudes toward aggression and paranoia. In order to understand the actions of an individual—to ascribe meaning, to appreciate motive, even to place proper value judgment on behavior—one must take into account the differing cultural directives that influenced it.

Cultural observation and generalization are risky but legitimate and necessary tools in sociological and psychological investigations. Here, rather than attempting my own defense of cultural generalizations, I will quote Primo Levi, who was himself profoundly victimized by such generalizations, yet became a penetrating student of them.

> I agree with you: it is dangerous, wrong, to speak about the "Germans," or any other people, as of a single undifferentiated entity, and include all individuals in one judgment. And yet I don't think I would deny that there exists a spirit of each people (otherwise it would not be a people), a *Deutschtum*, an *Italianita*, an *Hispanidad:* they are the sums of traditions, customs, history, language, and culture. Whoever does not feel within himself this spirit, which is national in the best sense of the word, not only does not belong to his own people but is not part of human civilization. Therefore, while I consider insensate the syllogism, "All Italians are passionate; you are Italian; therefore you are passionate," I do however believe it legitimate, within certain limits, to expect from Italians taken as a whole, or from Germans, or other nations, one specific, collective behavior rather than

another. There will certainly be individual exceptions, but a
prudent, probabilistic forecast is in my opinion possible.*

Some profound differences in moral values among different
cultures are justifiably a matter of opinion and open to debate.
Whether abortion, therapeutic cloning, arranged marriage, capital
punishment, paternalism—on all of which I have strong opinions—
are wrong or right is a proper area for legitimate differences. Decent people can disagree on many important issues without conceding the ethical ground. But there are not "two sides to every
question." With many questions there is only one morally accept-
able opinion. There are values that transcend cultural directives
and that must always be honored. Immoral behavior cannot be
exonerated on the grounds that it was influenced by an immoral
culture. He who subscribes to the values of a culture of evil is by
definition evil. The white Boers who ruled South Africa were
products of their environment. But apartheid was an evil practice, and the fact that Boers were raised in a racist environment
does not exempt their racist actions from condemnation.

We consider actions to be a product of an autonomous individual, even while acknowledging the power exerted by the culture
on that individual during his formative years. We may be sympa-
thetic to the individual, while still loathing his behavior. We do
not have to subscribe to moral relativism. We can insist that there
are universal goods and evils that transcend cultural differences.

Violation of those universal values must not be tolerated on
the basis of "cultural diversity." Slavery is wrong always. Racial
and religious persecution, child abuse, the subjugation of women,
torture, gratuitous cruelty (to people *or* animals), rape, and

---

*Primo Levi, *The Drowned and the Saved*, trans. R. Rosenthal (New York: Vin-
tage Books, 1989), pp. 183–84.

pederasty—to list but some—are never justifiable. Were a culture to espouse these values, we would then be perfectly free—morally obligated, I would say—to condemn it as pathological or evil.

We have a significant list of characteristics that by general agreement allow us to define a culture of hatred. The prime example in modern times, and perhaps in all history, is surely Nazi Germany. This is not to say that there have not been other monstrous events of mass slaughter and destruction in the past. But Germany in the twentieth century—with its newfound might and powers—created a Holocaust against the Jews that became the event that redefined that term. In its pathological assaults on the Jew, often to the detriment of its self-interest in the war; in its calculated and perverse technology of mass torture and killing; in its psychotic rationalizations; in its senseless cruelties; in the persistent and unremitting pursuit of genocide to the final moments of the war—Nazi Germany became the defining example of a culture of hatred.

How could the Holocaust have happened? How could such a monstrous policy have been initiated in a modern, highly educated, technological society, in so public a manner, with so little resistance from the outside world of passive onlookers, the *Zuschauenden*? In other words, why Germany, why the Jews, and what explains the passivity in the face of such evil by the Christian churches and the leaders of liberal democracy?* These are questions for all times and all disciplines. These are questions that result in multiple, but only partial, answers. Here, I use the Holocaust only as an extreme example to illustrate the *psychol-*

---

*To the immense literature of the Holocaust, in the past decade two books have been added that seriously approach the question from the standpoint of the bystander populations: Raul Hilberg, *Perpetrators Victims Bystanders* (New York: HarperPerennial, 1994) and Victoria J. Barnett, *Bystanders: Conscience and Complicity During the Holocaust* (Westport, Conn.: Praeger Press, 2000).

ogy of group hatred, without any pretense of explaining its historic meaning or political evolution.

Antisemitism

In an uncharacteristically overwrought article in *Esquire* magazine in 1974, Cynthia Ozick, the talented writer and brilliant social critic, declared that in the warmest of Christian hearts there is a cold place reserved for the Jews. This was in response to the fact that with the opening of Chinese society (then just happening), antisemitism seemed to be one of the first Western ideas to be heartily embraced by the Chinese, despite an obvious lack of any significant association with Jews. How could the Chinese so quickly adopt antisemitic stereotypes? One would normally expect, as Ozick clearly did, that some contact, some bad experiences, some history of animosity, must antedate a rancorous condemnation of an entire group.

A similar dejected feeling to that of Ozick's must have permeated the atmosphere at the Vidal Sassoon International Center for the Study of Antisemitism in Jerusalem, when they were made aware in 1994 of the presence in Japan and Korea of a "mystifyingly positive response to the antisemitic stereotype of the Jew found in the *Protocols of the Elders of Zion*"–a poisonous antisemitic tract then being actively circulated in Asia. These two countries are even more unlikely to have had any extensive experience with Jews than China.

The Jews are the quintessential scapegoats–the oldest pariah population, the most universally demonized people. Antisemitism has been traced back to earliest recorded history. And over the centuries, its ready recrudescence and the intensity of loathing and hatred that has been directed against the Jews have been astonishing.

The history of antisemitism is so well documented that one would expect nothing new could emerge. The literature is so imposing—more than thirty thousand volumes at the Sassoon Center—that one would assume little headway could be made by a new historian or sociologist approaching the subject. Yet each new emergence of militant antisemitism is a particularly lurid reminder of its ubiquitous presence and produces a rash of new analytic studies. The Holocaust, in its irrational extreme and terrifying results, ushered in a new era of scholarship on antisemitism and, arising in the post-Freudian era, offered new emphasis on its psychological aspects. Earlier attempts at psychological understanding had some perverse results.

In the wake of the Dreyfus Affair—an antisemitic outrage that rocked France at the end of the nineteenth century—a French Jewish journalist, Bernard Lazare, wrote his now-controversial but important book, *Antisemitism: Its History and Causes.** It is now controversial because the text is most likely to be quoted these days in antisemitic literature. It is important because it was a pioneering effort to understand the psychological foundations of antisemitism. The psychological underpinnings of antisemitism, as distinguished from its sociological and historical roots, are relevant to all forms of hatred.

The Jew haters have drawn comfort and ammunition particularly from Lazare's first chapter, which deals with general causes. In it he stated:

This race has been the object of hatred with all the nations amidst whom it ever settled. Inasmuch as the enemies of the Jews belonged to diverse races, as they dwelled far apart from one another, were ruled by different laws and governed by

*Bernard Lazare, *Antisemitism: Its History and Causes* (1894; reprint, Lincoln and London: University of Nebraska Press, 1995).

opposite principle; as they had not the same customs and
differed in spirit from one another, so they could not possibly
judge alike of any subject, it must need be that the general
causes of antisemitism have always resided in Israel itself [this
was written a half century before the creation of the state of
Israel, and therefore, "Israel" as used throughout Lazare's text
refers not to a state but to the Jews collectively], and not in those
who antagonized it.*

That statement has become a credo of antisemitic literature,
and the arguments that follow from it have led to an unfair labeling of Lazare by many as a Jewish antisemite. Nevertheless, he
continued in the very next—and less quoted—paragraph: "This
does not mean that justice was always on the side of Israel's per-
secutors, or that they did not indulge in all the extremes born of
hatred; it is merely asserted that the Jews were themselves, in
part, at least, the cause of their own ills."

As one follows Lazare's text, the source of the confusion becomes apparent. It stems from the ambiguity in his use of the
word "cause." We tend these days to use "cause" when we mean
"the agent that necessarily or ineluctably leads to a result." We
use "reason," a similar word, to refer to that which might "explain the occurrence or nature of an effect." Similarly we have
the word "occasion" to use for "a situation that permits or stimu-
lates existing causes to come into play." Although the victim population may seem to offer significant reasons and occasions for
their being targeted, they are *never* the cause.

Hatred, to be sustained as an ongoing relationship, is always
an attempt by the hater to deal with the humiliating and frustrating conditions of his own existence. The hater is attempting to
resolve an internal conflict and requires the victim population to

---

*Ibid., p. 8.

facilitate his displacement and rationalization. The only reason for examining victim populations is to find clues as to how they serve the unconscious machinations of the haters.

Still, the question remains in some minds whether there might not be legitimate grounds for hatred in which the victim shares responsibility. When we deal with group hatreds, we are often offered authentic grounds as rationalizations, particularly where there is a historic record of some barbaric action on the part of the victimized population. Time heals most of those wounds. Most Serbs did not spend their days obsessing about the genocidal assaults of the Croats in World War II. Even though a historic enmity had been established, both groups lived together as Yugoslavs. Of course hostilities remained, particularly since the atrocities were committed during the lifetime of the living generation. This hostility was readily capable of being revived in the power struggles that followed the dissolution of the Yugoslav state. Savage acts of hatred erupted, but under the stimulus and exploitation of a ruling group that found ready usage for such hatred.

Lazare, treading lightly as a Jew in a virulently antisemitic France, started his study with the contributions that the Jews may have made to antisemitism, although he then followed with a broad historic indictment of the bigots. As a product of a bigoted society, he did buy into antisemitic generalizations, as would his fellow student of French antisemitism, Jean-Paul Sartre a half century later.* Still, he assumed that something in the manner of Jews invites hatred.

---

*Sartre was accepting of the fact that Jews had "physical conformations that one encounters more frequently than among non-Jews." He clearly makes the point that the stereotype is not universal or exclusive to Jews. Still, it is disquieting to find this ardent champion of the Jews describing one of his friends as being of a marked semitic type: "He had a hooked nose, protruding ears, and

Lazare asked: "Which virtues or which vices have earned for the Jew this universal enmity: Why was he ill-treated and hated alike and in turn by the Alexandrians, by the Persians and the Arabs, by the Turks and the Christian nations: Because, everywhere up to our own days the Jew was an unsociable being."*

What did Lazare mean by this and what was the validity of his observation? He was observing correctly that the Jews in the Diaspora were a ubiquitous and generally unassimilated presence. Edward I in 1290 could make England the earliest *Judenrein* (Jew-free) country in Europe precisely because the Jews were a readily identifiable community within the larger one. They looked different and they behaved differently. One hardly would think to blame these thirteenth-century Jews for their "unsociability," unless one understands the argument Lazare used when he defined the term.

"Unsociability" as used by Lazare means the failure to adapt to the culture of the majority, not unfriendliness or rejecting behavior. In that argument he found three roots for the refusal of most Jews to assimilate: First, Jews do not submit to the rules of the conqueror the way other subject populations have, where a clear line existed between their "religious teachings which had come from the gods, and their civil laws."†

Judaism, unlike most other religions, is not simply a theological credo, but a set of civil laws that prescribe everyday rules for hygiene, morality, managing properties, conditions for worship and sacrifice. Obedience to these laws is not a choice but

---

thick lips. A Frenchman would have recognized him as a Jew without hesitation." Jean-Paul Sartre, *Anti-Semite and Jew*, tran. George J. Becker (New York: Schocken Books, 1965), p. 61.

*Lazare, *Antisemitism*, p. 9

†Lazare, *Antisemitism*, p. 9.

demanded by God. To maintain religious identity, the Jew must remain secularly isolated and distinguishably different, in conduct as well as appearance, from those around him or her.

Second, Lazare notes that Talmudic tradition sustains these civil injunctions through Halachic rule, the tradition insisting that observant Jews follow a prescribed code of conduct, thus resisting assimilation to the modes of the dominant civilization. To violate Talmudic tradition in any of its details is not stubbornness, it is a breach of covenant with the Lord.

Third, in the religious tradition of the landless Jews, the image of Jerusalem haunted them, demanding a return and making every other home and place a temporary one. Nothing is more destructive of grand theory than the working of time and history. Nineteenth-century France was the reality under which Lazare lived and set the conditions for his observations. Things changed in the twentieth century. The increasing pluralism of less homogeneous democracies such as the United States—while still not free of bigotry—offered latitude for diverse beliefs of an unparalleled nature. The emergence of Reform Judaism, born in nineteenth-century Germany, ironically, cast off many of the Talmudic codes of behavior, allowing for an extent of Jewish assimilation in the twentieth century not imaginable in the nineteenth. But to what avail? The new conditions allowed the German Jew to consider himself a German first and a Jew as a modifying subclass, that is, a Jewish German, but he would still be perceived by the Nazis as just another Jew who must be tortured and exterminated.

Later, the establishment of the state of Israel and the emergence of additional liberal forms of Judaism would completely destroy Lazare's third argument. Modern Jews in droves abandoned the messianic vision. They do not see redemption of their souls as requiring their presence in Jerusalem. Most modern Jews, not followers of an orthodoxy, replaced the idea of mes-

sianic redemption with the liberal cultural idea of leading a
moral life. Certainly this was the case with the German Jews, who
felt the first blows of the Holocaust.

Still Lazare acutely appreciated the basic conditions that have
made the Jews historic scapegoats. Judaism is not simply a religion, it is an identifiable culture, a people without a country.
(True, the state of Israel would reinvent the Jewish state, but to
what degree the Israeli culture is the culture of the Jew in the
Diaspora is still an open and intriguing question.)

Gordon Allport, the brilliant American psychologist, wrote *The
Nature of Prejudice* a half century ago. It remains the most profound book on the subject yet written. Still, in the post-
Holocaust era, with his deep humanism, he hedged on the
reasons for antisemitism:

> Anti-Semitism arises because people are irritated by their own
> consciences. Jews are symbolically their superego, and no one
> likes to be ridden so hard by his superego. Ethical conduct is
> insisted upon by Judaism, relentlessly, immediately, hauntingly.
> People who dislike this insistence, along with the self-discipline
> and acts of charity implied, are likely to justify their rejection by
> discrediting the whole race that produced such high ethical
> ideals.*

To think of Judaism as simply a religious choice like Method-
ism or Unitarianism is to deny the historic meaning of a people.
The Jew is the stranger, the disbeliever, the alien—not at your
border but in your streets and in your presence. It is not the
"high ethical ideals" that offend the antisemites, it is the Jew's
ubiquity. Jews are everywhere, everywhere a minority (Israel

---

*Gordon W. Allport, *The Nature of Prejudice* (New York: Doubleday Anchor
Books, 1958), p. 242.

excepted), and everywhere identifiable. Their identity is marked not just by their beliefs, but by their very behavior and the practices that sustained those beliefs over the ages—circumcision, dietary laws, Sabbath celebrations, and special historic and religious holidays. These practices—embraced by them as a proud cultural heritage—confront the common Christian culture and its most profound religious beliefs. Jews reject the figure of Christ and deny the revealed truth of the New Testament. For the Jew there is no *new* testament. The very term is anathema to Orthodox Jews, who see in it a rejection of the Scriptures, the very word of God. The name "Old Testament" was indeed coined by Christians and many Jews are careful not to use that term.

In most cultures this denial has been perceived as a stubborn arrogance; a rejection of the customs of the host country; and, particularly offensive, a rejection of the new religion. To some devout Christians, not only do the Jews reject Christ, but they also killed him. And in much of the Christian world, antisemitism has had strong support—even encouragement—from the moral authorities of the Church. The powerful rationalizing effect of such moral authority—exactly like the rationalizing effect of a delusion—gives legitimacy to bigotry. Moreover, it lends passion to bigotry, converting it into hatred. The Nazis had generations of cultural and religious hatred of Jews to draw on when they launched their genocidal assault.

Nazi Germany

The Nazis did not arbitrarily select the Jews rather than Sunni Muslims or the Zen Buddhists. The Nazis emerged from a European and Christian culture and were influenced by their location and historic traditions. Antisemitism was evident in Europe from the beginnings of the Diaspora in the sixth century B.C. Even the greatest of the classical writers—Cicero, Juvenal, Ovid, Pliny, Seneca, and Tacitus—all managed to embroider their works with antisemitic observations. But antisemitism never had the central role in the classical period that it would gain with the rise of Christianity.

Greek and Roman culture had the same contempt for early Christians—perhaps more—that it had for the Jews. It was only with the ascendance of Christianity that the Jews were perceived as the primal enemy within, the living symbols of the rejection of the Christ. The antisemitism built into Church writings and Church attitudes accompanied the spread of Christianity throughout Europe. The Nazis, despite their own rejection of Christianity, would exploit the traditional Christian antisemitic stereotypes dormant in most of the cultures of Europe.

The Nazis found rationalizing arguments for their assault on the Jews in the tradition of antisemitism laced throughout the theology of the New Testament and the writings of the Christian churches in Europe. Robert S. Wistrich, a distinguished scholar of antisemitism, pointed out the easy pathways and respectable rationalizations that were readily available to Nazi propagandists in the traditions of the Christian religion.

He noted that there was the rich strain of antisemitism central to the Gospels, themselves, where the Jews are depicted as "as a pariah people, as the murderers of Christ . . . in league with Satan himself." And the Nazis drew on teachings of the Church Fathers, who persistently referred to Jews as slanderers, blasphemers, an accursed people. Even the most saintly of Christian fathers—Augustine, Ambrose, Jerome, and Cyril—saved "a cold spot in their hearts" for the Jews. Luther, fully embracing the traditional antisemitism of the Catholic church he was rejecting, would offer even further religious justifications for demonizing the Jews.

Wistrich said, "The Nazi hierarchy was laden with paranoid

Jew haters. The Nazis exploited and secularized familiar religious images of the Jew as Host desecrators, demons, sorcerers, well poisoners, and ritual murderers—as usurers, infidels, and insatiable conspirators seeking the destruction of Christian society."*

Demonizing the Jews—an essential ingredient of hatred toward them—came naturally to the Nazi leaders. Hitler, Himmler, Goebbels, and many others in the Nazi leadership truly believed in the demonic and vile Jew. They did not cynically invent a myth for the masses. They offered the *Volk* what was already in their hearts. The secular religion called Nazism, in its selection of an enemy and victim, successfully drew on the centuries of anti-semitism endemic in Christian theology and teaching.

In a religious community, the image of the Jews as the devil incarnate, the anti-Christ, formed an effective means of demonizing them. One could attack the Jews as the forces of evil and label their persecution a noble pursuit and a religious obligation. But in a perverse way, this image of the Jews enhances them. The devil is admittedly the force of evil, but he is a force. He is superhuman. In Nazi philosophy, the role of the superhuman is reserved for the Aryan hero. The Jew must be a creature less than human.

The Germans went beyond demonizing in their particularly virulent form of antisemitism. The Jews were not just evil people. *They were not people.* They were subhuman. They were parasites.

The rules of behavior are changed when one moves from dealing with humans, even evil humans, to lesser creatures. To make the Jew into an animal is to remove him from the limits of protection afforded even the vilest of humans. Most countries these days do not execute even their most feared and detested criminals. People shoot animals, however, just for sport. And if animals

---

*Robert S. Wistrich, "The Devil, the Jews, and Hatred of the 'Other,'" in *Demonizing the Other*, ed. Wistrich (Jerusalem: Harwood Academic Publishers, 1999), p. 3.

are a threat to us—a rabid dog—we are not just permitted, but obliged, to kill it.

The Nazis found the most effective means of dehumanizing: The Jew would be viewed not just as an animal, but as the lowest form, a parasite. People may romanticize dogs, but no one finds affection for a tubercle bacillus or a smallpox virus. The Jews, who started out as well poisoners—spreaders of disease—now became the disease itself. Hitler, himself, had introduced the idea of the Jew as parasite in *Mein Kampf,* where the analogy is used throughout. Nazi publications characteristically referred to the Jew as bacteria, scum, tuberculosis, cancer, maggots, and viruses.

In his diary for March 27, 1942, Joseph Goebbels wrote: "The Jews will destroy us if we do not defend ourselves against them. This is a war of life or death between the Aryan race and the Jewish virus."*

This statement encapsulates almost all the elements that are central to the definition of a paranoid state: (1) It differentiates an us from a them, defining two alternative cultures. (2) It defines the "other" as an enemy. We are obsessed with the enemy who now becomes part of our daily life. (3) It identifies a life-threatening situation, thereby justifying eradication of the enemy as an act of self-defense. (4) It dehumanizes the enemy, identifying him as a virus, thereby denying him his right to the normal protections accorded "our fellow men." We may respond with satisfaction at the sight of the piled corpses accumulated in the killing fields as a job well done, as an exterminator would respond at a mound of destroyed rats in a garbage dump, as many in the Arab world delight at viewing the results of a suicide bombing.

---

*Goebbels was minister of propaganda under Hitler. As quoted by Yisrael Gutman, "On the Character of Nazi Antisemitism," in Shmuel Almog, *Antisemitism Through the Ages*, tran. Nathan Eisner (Oxford: Pergamon Press, 1988), p. 369.

The sheer intensity and murderous rage of the Nazis eventually transcended all rationalization, taking antisemitism to an extreme and insane end. Robert Wistrich labeled the Nazi hatred of the Jews as a singularly irrational event even in the irrational world of bigotry. What made it remarkable to him was the fact that the Nazis' pathological pursuit of the Jews was independent of Jewish actions or belief:

> Nazi racism sought to annihilate Jews not for what they did, for their faith, their customs, or political opinions, but for what they were alleged to be, for their very *being*. The fatality of birth condemned Jews to death, every Jew and all Jews, everywhere and always. They were the counter-type, the paradigmatic "other" race inassimilable by definition, inclassable [sic], outside the natural hierarchy of races, beyond the human pale. Not even a race, strictly speaking (since they were "unnatural"), perverse, demonic, the intrinsically evil "other"—in a word, the Jews were the Devil incarnate in human form. Their extermination—in the worldview of Nazi zoological racism—was the prerequisite not simply to secure German race-purity and "Aryan" hegemony, but ultimately the happiness of all mankind.*

The insane hatred of the Jews by Hitler and his henchmen was rooted in their individual pathologies, but to accomplish their goals, they required the cooperation of the majority of an entire nation. The intensity of hatred necessary to mobilize that population in support of the Holocaust could not be based on historic data. It had to be in the here and now. It was the job of the psychopathic and psychotic Nazi leadership to supply rational reasons to the population, which was not itself preponderantly composed of psychotic members, in order to gain the people's

---

*Wistrich, p. 4

cooperation for what objectively can be only viewed as an insane obsession. The Nazi propagandists justified the genocide of the Jews by equating it as we treat our "war on cancer" or, more accurately, our successful campaigns to eliminate smallpox and poliomyelitis. To succeed, to protect the future of their children, they had to destroy the virus to the very last presence on earth. This was to be a universal genocide.

Daniel Goldhagen, while acknowledging that the Nazi leaders represented a degree of pathology unparalleled in modern history, held that the German people were particularly receptive to adoption of so paranoid a view of the Jews. Even before the rise of the Nazis, he claimed, the German people were possessed of a particularly virulent form of antisemitism; they viewed the Jews as biologically different, a race apart. Since, according to the Germans, the Jewish characteristics that they perceived were rooted in genetics, as distinguished from culture, the Jews' evil ways were immutable. Worse, they could be transmitted through generations, and transmitted to purer races. The Jews, all Jews, had to be destroyed. It was a matter of survival for the German people; the Holocaust was an act of self-defense.*

There is a certain reassurance in feeling that a culture of hatred requires such special conditions as Goldhagen outlined: (1) a ruthless and mad leadership; (2) seizing power in a geomilitary situation specific to Germany; and (3) acting out on a particularly susceptible population, the German people. One can take comfort in this hypothesis. It makes the possibility of a recurrence of a horror like the Holocaust that much less likely.

While I remain admiring of Goldhagen's understanding of the mechanisms of hatred, I do not think he made the case that Nazism could only have been a German phenomenon. I am not

---

*Daniel J. Goldhagen, *Hitler's Willing Executioners: Ordinary Germans and the Holocaust* (New York: Knopf, 1996).

convinced that the Germans were more virulently antisemitic than the Poles, the Lithuanians, the Ukrainians, or the French, for that matter. Jedwabne certainly indicates the capacity of the Poles to treat Jews as disposable scum. And while much has been made of the danger posed by the eugenics movement that swept Germany in the 1920s, eugenics was taken seriously in most of the Western world—in the United States particularly—without leading to political policies of racial engineering, let alone genocide. "Genetic engineering," when discussed in the United States, is limited to the context of medical cures or improvement of agricultural products, not in the preservation of the purity of the race.

A culture of hatred is not necessarily a culture of haters. At least it may not start out that way. Even were every German an antisemite, which we know was not the case, prejudice is still not hatred. The typical antisemite is not an active Jew hater. Like any typical racist, he is relatively unconcerned about the disdained population. He stereotypes them, denigrates them, and for the most part ignores them. He may be a bigot, concerned with protecting himself from the contamination of the pariah population in his clubs and community, even in his schools. He may take pleasure in their humiliation, but he is not preoccupied with them. He wants less involvement, not more. His sin is in his exclusion of an individual from his concerns and compassion on the basis of his prejudice. But a bigot is an easy mark and a ready follower of those who hate. The immense value of Goldhagen's book is in its demonstration of the capacity of a paranoid leadership to convert a mass population to "willing executioners." All that such leadership needs to expedite its purposes is the absolute power of dictatorship and the precondition of a prejudice within the population.

The Nazi battle against the Jews illustrates another danger that the autocratic state poses for the world at large. Antisemitism was endemic in Europe and much of the rest of the world. For centuries it was actively encouraged. Before the Nazis indicated the malevolence that could be unleashed by such latent bigotry, most people tolerated—some enjoyed—the smarmy statements of prejudice and occasional brutal acts of individual bigotry. Until the Holocaust, we were unaware that a determined cadre of haters could ignite latent prejudice and bigotry into a conflagration that might consume us all. But now we see how such bigotry has been used by despots in Iraq, Libya, and Cambodia to consolidate their tenuous hold on their subject populations. They displace the authentic resentment of their deprived populations and divert it to manufactured enemies abroad. This technique—mastered by Saddam Hussein, Muammar al-Khadafy, Pol Pot, and their ilk—to subjugate their own people now threatens the security of the entire world. Such leadership must be confronted by the more civilized nations of the world.

But now there are enemies beyond the traditional national ones, occupying communities without boundaries. Osama bin Laden is the leader of a community of haters, Al Qaeda. But where can we locate either bin Laden or his community?

13

A COMMUNITY OF HATERS

Germany is a country with boundaries, a history, culture, and a common language. In other words, it is a nation. Its national characteristics differ significantly from that of other cultures. This is apparent after spending even one night in Tokyo and Berlin. The people look different and comport themselves differently. Cultural attitudes differ significantly even among such neighboring countries with overlapping ethnicity as France, Italy, and Switzerland. Even within the borders of a single country there are subcommunities whose occupants display different forms of behavior, dictated by that subculture. The fast pace and aggressive attitude one finds in New York are significantly different from the laid-back style of Santa Fe. While there is an American culture that binds us in familiarity, these subcultures shape multiple variants of the American character. I certainly experienced a sense of cultural confusion on first moving to New York from the Midwest.

A community of haters, on the other hand, is not a community in the traditional sense of a group defined by a shared geography, politics, or culture. It is an affinity group brought together and emotionally bonded by the shared passion of its members. Formed in different ways, a community of haters operates under different conditions. The culture of hatred is a culture converted to hatred in order to serve the political agenda of its leadership. The community of haters is a group of disparate individuals who find one another and band together because of their shared passion.

Joined in a Web of Hatred

The Aryan Nation in the United States and its ideological counterparts in Europe, the skinheads, are affinity groups. They are communities of haters. Earth Liberation Front is such a community. To a significant degree, so is Al Qaeda. These people are joined one to the other by a common passion. The members of Al Qaeda, for example, form a transnational community of poverty, feudalism, and despair. The frustration at their stagnant and depressed state in the face of rapid progress of neighboring communities must be controlled by their leadership. It is handled by diverting their anger from their national oppressors and directing it toward a scapegoat—the international Jewish and American conspiracy.

Al Qaeda is a classic group defined by its beliefs. It makes them a community in ideology, if not geography. And it is a dangerous community. It has demonstrated that once the community of ideas has been created, it is easy for smaller terrorist cells dispersed geographically to be mobilized to carry out common policies of the larger network.

Nothing facilitates the identification of like individuals and their merger into groups as the modern technologies of communications, from radio to the worldwide web. Technology has made possible the creation of global communities of ideology. The rapid changes that marked the latter half of the twentieth century were almost exclusively in the area of communications. These advances have dramatically shrunk the geophysical world, creating one massive interconnected community, ripe for the transmission of ideas and capable of calling to action similar-minded people in disparate and unlikely places. It has made possible ideological communities that cut across national boundaries and interests.

There is a tendency to miss the singularity of this brave new world of ideology, which creates communities without borders. The spread of cellular telephones, global television, Internet access, and the common languages of computers allows ideas to suffuse the globe in moments. These days, the universal word that everyone seems to understand is not the word of God—who seems to whisper different messages into the ears of his self-chosen messengers—but the Word of Microsoft. And the language spoken is English for the most part.

Neither Max Scheler, at the turn of the nineteenth century, nor Gordon Allport, in the 1940s, two major scholars of bigotry and prejudice, anticipated the new sense of community created by the communications revolution and what it would mean. Both assumed that hatred was likely to emerge in heterogeneous societies and democracies that promised more than they deliver. And both were dealing with prejudice, not obsessive hatred.

Scheler was convinced that prejudice stemmed from the discrepancy between the political promise of power to a group of citizens and its actual power. He was thinking in terms of a country, a democratic country at that, where a group of citizens saw promises unkept and equality denied. Such a group would be resentful of any other groups that seemed to be flourishing at its expense. It could harbor a righteous rage at their leaders, but to

change leaders might require revolution, and revolution is difficult. Instead, it could identify a victim minority that seemed to be
stealing its birthright. Scheler—writing a full generation before
they occurred—anticipated the conditions of Germany in the
1930s.

Allport listed ten conditions for prejudice to prevail. It required a society:

> Where the social structure is marked by heterogeneity
> Where vertical mobility is permitted
> Where rapid social change is in progress
> Where there are ignorance and barriers to communication
> Where the size of a minority group is large or increasing
> Where direct competition and realistic threats exist
> Where exploitation sustains important interests in the
>   community
> Where customs regulating aggression are favorable to bigotry
> Where traditional justifications for ethnocentrism are
>   available
> Where neither assimilation nor cultural pluralism is favored*

Both Scheler and Allport were thinking in terms of geographical communities, and they had in mind Western democracies like
Germany and the United States. None of the six first conditions
in Allport's list is present in Saudi Arabia, Pakistan, Indonesia,
Iraq, Syria, Afghanistan, or most of the Islamic states from which
Al Qaeda draws its loyalties. Neither author envisioned the kind
of ideological community that transcends physical boundaries,
the kind of community that became possible only in the new age
of communication.

---

*Gordon W. Allport, *The Nature of Prejudice* (Garden City, N.Y.: Doubleday Anchor Book, 1958), pp. 215–16.

Isolated and alien haters spread across an increasingly shrinking globe can now find their emotional counterparts in lands they barely knew existed. Furthermore, the disparity between their existence and that of people in the developed nations—once only barely appreciated—can now be visualized in all its plush and plentiful detail. The impoverished Afghans or Palestinians in refugee camps can view on television the good life that others enjoy in different and distant societies, leading to feelings of unfairness and envy. And of course such disparity in the human condition is monumentally unfair. Such people can then be convinced that their misery is part of a zero-sum game that is necessary to support the indulgences of a rich society like the United States.

The cynical leaders of these depressed communities encourage such displacement in order to divert the frustrated rage away from the even more extreme inequities at home, where gilt palaces coexist with mud houses. The enmity between Sunni and Shiite, Iraq and Iran, can be put on hold while all join in unity supporting Al Qaeda. This group cuts across national boundaries and creates a true community of haters bonded by their shared envy and intense hatred of that great Satan, the United States of America. Why the United States? Who else represents all that they desire, all that they are entitled to? In the world of paranoia and projection, he who has what you have not has taken it from you.

What distinguishes the hatred of the Al Qaeda from the hatred manifest in the Palestinian refugee camps is that with the latter there is an actual geographical community and a territorial enemy to be joined with an ideological one. Still, the nature of the hatred is the same.

Hatred is always an attempt to find a way of dealing with one's impotent rage before it strangles one. Hatred is designed to make reason of one's agony and frustration. It is an attempt to convert humiliation into pride. Hatred among the Palestinians is an attempt to find rationality out of the inequity of their conditions and that of their neighbors in Israel. The Israelis exist in a state that—by its sharp contrasts—mocks the conditions of their Arab neighbors. They are a high-tech, democratic state that illuminates all the true deprivations of the vast majority of the Arabs in the Middle East from Egypt to Iran. And with the emergence of an almost steady state of war, actual grievances support the biases of the Arabs.

The Israelis are but a pygmy, however, in comparison with the American colossus that bestrides the real world. Hostility towards the American Goliath is seeping into the cultures of such European democracies as France and Germany, which feel eclipsed and less respected, less "equal." Unilateral actions by the United States, of course, do not help. If resentment against the United States exists in such similar states—with allies bonded by two world wars—what can one expect from the disenfranchised? Because of its strength and its riches, United States has become a target for the envy of all the oppressed Muslim communities from Africa to Asia. Al Qaeda taps that envy to create a community of haters that ignores the local political conditions, which clearly separate the interests of the disadvantaged groups. Hatred for the United States can make allies out of Iran and Iraq.

While the inequities between Israel and the United States, on the one hand, and these deprived communities, on the other, are real, the ascribed cause of the inequities is manufactured out of convenience. It is easier to blame the other rather than one's own. It is the cynical leadership of Syria, Iran, Iraq, and the Palestinians that control their people and deprive them of a richer life in a modern world. But that same leadership controls the media and the schools that will determine the perceptions of the underprivileged. It is that leadership that will find the scapegoat.

To the Palestinians, the Israelis are invaders occupying land that the Palestinians view as rightly theirs. But the latter's readiness to displace their rage onto innocent Jewish targets around the world exposes an anti-Jewish bigotry that contaminates what well may have been considered authentic and righteous rage. The antisemitic hatred is facilitated by the radicalism and bias of Islamic preachers who declare all Jews infidels, all Jews enemies, all Jews suitable for attack.

Independent of just and rational debates about the differing claims of the Palestinians and their Arab supporters and the Israelis, the two peoples now differ in psychological terms. The Palestinians have become a community of hatred and the Israelis have not. I am not here entering the debate about who has victimized whom; of where historic fairness lies; of right and wrong. I am not making a case of who has necessarily inflicted the most pain or has done the greater injustice. I am not even measuring the bigotry of one group compared with the other. I am talking of the emerging psyches.

The Palestinians daily demonstrate, in their actions and words, their delight at the sight of the macerated victims of suicide bombers and their pride in the bombers. The Israelis, even when they have clearly committed atrocities, have struggled with shame and angry denial, not self-congratulations (this may be changing with time and frustration, particularly among the ultra-Orthodox Jewish settlers). The reasons for hatred lie in the degraded nature of the life of most Palestinians in a modern world that owes them more. The have-nots are always more likely to be involved in mass hatred than the haves. Unfortunately, even the haves may perceive themselves as have-nots—witness the leadership of Al Qaeda. What is "not had" is respect, not just money. Francis Bacon in his superb essay on envy linked deprivation to general causes of envy:

Men's minds will either feed upon their own good or upon
others' evil; and who wanteth the one will prey upon the other;

and whoso is out of hope to attain to another's virtue will seek to come at even hand by depressing another's fortune. . . . He that cannot possibly mend his own case will do what he can to impair another. . . . [This] is the case of men that rise after calamities and misfortunes. For they are as men fallen out with the times, and think other men's harms a redemption of their own sufferings.*

The Arab world is a community of people "fallen out with the times."

The Power of Religion

The typical community of haters is formed through their allegiance to a common cause—the unborn, the environment, helpless animals—and a common enemy. While the community is often strident, its major danger comes from those at the fringe of the movement ready to act out their own despair in the service of a legitimate cause. It is an assemblage of the converted. It has relatively little opportunity to evangelize a larger population

The radical Islamic movement is different. It, too, is a transnational group linking like-minded people. But Islam is a natural constituency of people joined by history, culture, and authentic beliefs. It is one of the major religions of our world. It starts with a following already unified in their identification one with the other. Radical Islamism is a major threat to world stability because of its ability to *create* hatred by converting normal populations of individuals into crusaders for a cause. Typical hatemongers do not have an existing constituency. They do not have

---

*Francis Bacon, "Of Envy," in *Francis Bacon: A Selection of His Works*, ed. Sidney Warhaft (New York: Macmillan, 1965), pp. 64–65.

the reach, or the authority, of religion. They cannot both direct and legitimate violence in a large community in the way that the mullahs of radical Islam have done. Religion has historically provided a fertile field for the definition of enemies and the creation of hatred. It is a traditional venue for the sponsorship of hatred.

It is unfashionable these days to implicate religious orthodoxies for their role in cultivating and disseminating hatred. We are a culture of tolerance and diversity, and we strive to protect ourselves from religious bigotry and hatred. But political correctness must contend with historic data. It is not just coincidence that when we examine the environments of persistent hatred such as Northern Ireland, the Balkans, the Indian subcontinent, and the Middle East, religious differences define the opposing populations, even where territory may be the ultimate aim.

Whenever religion is involved—whether for purposes of conversion or conquest—the name and power of God will be invoked in justification of all actions. Religious leaders, since the First Crusade and even before, have motivated the masses with the same promises that the mullahs use in encouraging Al Qaeda. Urban II promised absolution of sins and financial support for the families of crusader heroes. The mullahs promise instant admission to the kingdom of heaven and supply monetary rewards to the families of suicide bombers. The battle cry of the First Crusade, supplied by the pope himself, was "Deus volt"—God wills it, setting historic precedent for the battle cry of the terrorists: "Allah be praised."

The individual paranoid must oppose his culture in insisting that he has been chosen personally by God, and in claiming that he hears the voice of God. He has to go through the psychic distortion of forming a delusion. No such radical suspension of reality is required of modern terrorists. Their religious leaders, who presume to speak for God, offer their followers an alternative to the delusion formation required of the paranoid.

The arbiters of many orthodox religions, whether Jewish, Christian, or Muslim, have arrogated to themselves the right to interpret the word of God in all areas of life, secular as well as religious. They have been granted this authority by the masses who willingly accept their authority. If the mullah indicates that a woman must be stoned to death for bearing a child out of wedlock, it will be done "in the name of Allah." The faithful will respond to those who are the interpreters of the word of Allah. They supply the voice of God to the nonpsychotic. This authority is a powerful alternative to delusion formation, which is a device only available to the psychotics among us.

Hatred for the devil has always been one hallmark of love of God. Those obsessed with hatred of evil, and apprised of the identity of the agents of evil, need generate no delusions to rationalize their hatred. The mass population, eager for some justification for their deprivation, is directed to viewing the United States as a prime example of the hand of Satan operating through the imperialist state. In addition, the people see on television the sinful lifestyle of the infidel that is so tempting to their children. Encouraged by the assurances of their religious leaders, they supply their children with an alternative passion. The ticket to the better life is a suicide mission. The child's place in paradise is assured, and their parents will find increased comforts at home supplied by benefactors from Iran and Iraq. They pursue and extinguish the enemy at the behest of their religious leaders and with the reassurance that planting a bomb in a school will be serving their God. No ideological leaders besides the religious ones have this enormous leverage.

Religions, or their ultranationalist equivalents, have the power to choose and identify "enemies." They do so by defining evil or heretic populations: Jews, Irish Protestants/Catholics, Serbs/Croats, Muslims/Hindus. Genocide sanctioned by dogma or orthodoxy and rationalized by political leaders can then be declared a means of purification, a defense of principle—in the service of God or the good—and even an act of survival. Religious leaders have enormous special powers to influence the believer far beyond that afforded secular leaders.

First, religion has "the Word." The prestige of the Church bureaucracy resides in its self-appointed position as intermediary between God and his subjects. Their authority is both interpretive and directive. Most of us do not hear the voice of God and are not privy to his wants. The power of religious leaders resides in their arrogation of the capacity and right to interpret the divine text.

Second, the Church is an educator. The Church bureaucracy, in its self-perpetuated role as interpreter of the divine text—whether the Koran or the Bible—arrogates a responsibility to inform and instruct the layman. The word of God is what the leaders say it is. They define the appropriate beliefs and the proper code of conduct. As God's instruments, religious leaders are regarded with the kind of fear and awe that inspire obedience. We now have a culturally accepted alternative to paranoid delusion, a method of receiving instructions from God and following his commandments. This power allows religious leaders to locate the source of misery in the populace; define the enemy, the infidel or the anti-Christ; and command action, whether crusade, jihad, or an act of personal martyrdom.

Third, faith supplies power. It demands allegiance and obedience beyond the tests of reason. Faith is demanded in most religious observers. One suspension of reason can facilitate the next. If one believes that Moses literally received the tablets of the law from God on Mount Sinai, then one is prepared to accept the delivery of the golden plates of the Book of Mormon to Joseph Smith in Palmyra, New York. And one can believe that the

Reverend Jim Jones will lead us out of the modern wilderness.* We unfairly denigrate the faith of believers in new religions, but the same suspension of logic is required in the traditional religions. The miracles of the Old and New Testaments would seem strange indeed if newly presented in the twenty-first century.

The power of faith is in its ability to counter all the impulses of instinct and the directives of rational thinking. Even the ubiquitous fear of death can be overcome by the promises of faith, whether through fusion with Christ, enshrinement in Valhalla, or admission to the earthly paradise, with its corporal and carnal pleasures, promised by Islam.

Finally, religion supplies passion. Religion (or ultranationalism) does more than define the enemy and rationalize the hatred. It supplies the passion. The kind of passion that allows for torture and cruelty is borrowed from religious ecstasy. Very little besides terror, sexual passion, or religious fervor can support the excesses of group hatred. The passion supplied by religion sustains hatred over a lifetime and across generations. The institution of religion is particularly well endowed with all the ingredients necessary to supply the tinder that ignites group hatred.

Another traditional role of religion that has made it useful to secular authorities is its ability to bring comfort to the masses, and comfort may be used in the service of civil control. Since life for the masses has historically been one of misery and toil, often because of exploitation by the privileged minority, the comfort offered by religion can serve as an emollient to the masses, making misery tolerable. One argument for the ready acceptance by secular powers of an alternative and potentially competitive leadership, the Church, has been the usefulness of religion in stabilizing a feudal and exploitative state. The promise of an afterlife

---

*In 1977, James Warren Jones led 1,000 of his followers to Jonestown, Guyana. In 1978, 911 of them committed mass suicide at his behest.

makes the here and now more bearable. Poverty may be endurable, even preferable, if it is true that the meek shall inherit the earth, and the poor man find justice in heaven.

For years, one of the intended or incidental effects of culturally sanctioned antisemitism in the Catholic and medieval cultures of Europe was the stabilizing effect it offered the state. The Church encouraged the perpetuation of antisemitism, "the longest hatred,"* for its utilitarian effects. The value of the Jews as scapegoats was in their capacity to divert the masses from the proper sources of their despair, a miserable and impoverished existence. This status quo was easy to maintain when the Church was powerful and unified, the states were weak and diverse, and there was no powerful middle class.

With the Reformation, the creation of the modern state, and the rise of a bourgeoisie, the balance shifted. The power of the universal Church was diminished. Diverse "truths" were revealed. The nation materialized as an alternative source of power, an alternative allegiance, and a new community of identification. After the separation of Church and state, rival loyalties were offered to the masses—Church and state—with diminished powers for each, or variable apportioning of the areas of power between the two, depending on the specific culture.

Out of the masses emerged a strong middle class with the kind of secular life that would be less easy to sacrifice for the admittedly grander, but less certain, future in heaven.† As life approximated in richness the qualities ascribed to an afterlife, it would

---

*This term is borrowed from the subtitle of *Antisemitism: The Longest Hatred,* ed. by Robert S. Wistrich and Fred Jordan (New York: Pantheon, 1991).

†Max Weber, the great sociologist, linked these diverse events in his classic book, *Protestant Ethic and the Spirit of Capitalism,* trans. Peter Baehr and Gordon C. Wells (New York: Penguin Classics, 2002), written in 1920 and translated into English in 1930.

be harder to abandon that which we know—the bird in the hand—for that which was only promised. Still, conditions would arise where a population filled with frustration, resentment, and despair would be ripe and waiting for an explosion into hatred. Max Scheler labeled this emotional state as *ressentiment,* and he described it as a dangerous, pathological, and destructive condition. *Ressentiment* is not exactly translatable to resentment, as it is more powerful than that, a toxic brew of resentment, envy, spite, rage, and revenge: "*Ressentiment* can only arise if these emotions are particularly powerful and yet must be suppressed because they are coupled with the feeling that one is unable to act them out—either because of weakness, physical or mental, or because of fear."*

Scheler described this condition as endemic in the Germany of 1912 in which he was writing. Twenty years or so later, the conditions were only intensified. In the period following the massive defeat of Germany in World War I, a nation emerged that was joined in humiliation and impoverishment. With the coming to power of a paranoid leadership—obsessed with a virulent anti-semitism born out of the leaders' individual psyches—a new Germany emerged. Democracy was replaced with a Fascist dictatorship. The pathological leaders offered a paranoid justification for the feelings of the Germans that relieved them of responsibility and supplied them with a culpable enemy. The qualities of both religion and statehood were combined under the Nazis. And then to supply passion and justification, a religious and mystical mission was offered. A crusade was initiated with the emphasis on protecting not just the people or the state but the purity of the Aryan "race." The Holocaust became a reality.

Ultranationalist dictatorships share certain characteristics of religious orthodoxy but these qualities are joined with the mili-

---

*Max Scheler, *Ressentiment* (New York: Schocken Books, 1972), p. 48.

tary powers of the state. When one combines the two, as is so common now in the Arab world, it becomes apparent why the Islamic state is now viewed as a center for international terrorism.

The work of Al Qaeda, the ideological community, is also supported by its fundamentalist assumptions. It is supported in its efforts by the existence of theocratic dictatorships throughout the Middle East, which erase the traditional balance of power between national and religious interests, limiting the excesses of either. With Al Qaeda the role of religion is central and all-powerful. Religion creates, encourages, rationalizes, and supports hatred—and supplies enemies, the infidel. Al Qaeda is particularly effective in its capacity to wreak havoc because it attaches its religious fanaticism to political struggles, operating as both a political movement and a religious crusade.

Al Qaeda has been described as the Muslim version of the Christian Crusades. The comparison is grossly inexact. The assumption is that because the Crusades represented the particular ideologies of a religion—the Christians—it was an ideological action. It was, in fact, a territorial one. When Pope Urban II gave his clarion call at the Council of Clermont in 1095, his purposes were clear. The object was not conversion of the heathen, but the liberation of the Holy Sepulcher in Jerusalem. It is generally agreed that the primary mission of the Church was gaining access to the holy places, whereas the promise of power and wealth motivated the secular leaders who actually mobilized the troops and initiated the actions. One of the major positive consequences of the Crusades was the creation of a larger community of interests and contact. The world of the West was enlarged, enriched, and complicated by its exposure to the East.

The modern networks of communication facilitated the formation of Al Qaeda. But what is the articulated purpose of this crusade? What is its Holy Sepulcher? What does Al Qaeda *want?* The easy answer is the security of a Palestinian state. That certainly is the goal of the Palestinian terrorist. But Al Qaeda is not motivated by the establishment of something. It is the destruction of something that Al Qaeda wants. But what is it? Some would say the destruction of the state of Israel. But the evidence and the chronology of their activities belie that. When they began to mention Israel, it seemed to come only as an afterthought. Destroying Israel appears to be an opportunistic claim, a Johnny-come-lately plan. Their true venom seems to be more directed to Jews in general as representative of the larger host of infidels.

Al Qaeda leaders, by embracing a general antisemitism, have now joined a traditional bigotry. They have found the one-size-fits-all enemy, the Jews. They send tanker trucks to destroy a Jewish synagogue in Tunisia and people with bombs to destroy Jewish cultural institutions in France. Israel appears to be a temporary convenience for Al Qaeda, a rationalization created to influence the liberal communities of Europe that have been offended by the Israeli occupation of the West Bank, and impatient at the lack of progress in a peace settlement. Israel is most likely a way station for Al Qaeda in its jihad against the hated modern state.

One suspects that the attacks on Jewish (not Israeli) targets in Europe and North Africa represent a temporary and safer alternative to the "Jewish schools and neighborhoods in the United States" that Al Qaeda indicated were to be its prime targets. And what perfect targets! By assaulting these American-Jewish institutions, it would threaten both the security of Jews in the United States and the country itself. That would join the surrogate, the Jews, to the great Satan that really offends it, the United States.

What is special about either Jews or Americans? Nothing. All infidels, all unbelievers, constitute Al Qaeda's theoretical enemy. But it is difficult to mobilize hatred toward so large and amorphous an enemy. Focus is necessary in a crusade. These two groups represent the most convenient entry points for Al Qaeda's hatred.

Al Qaeda represents the new community of hatred, as Nazi Germany represented the old. Traditional hatred has always been stoked by rage. And rage has been triggered by fear. Both are the products of feeling humiliated and threatened. Traditional hatred was built on competition for food, land, and survival. The enemy is at our gates; it is them or us. The savage hatred and barbarity manifest between the Iroquois and their enemies, the neighboring and related tribes during the American colonial period, were a product of that special animus often reserved for neighbors and brothers. The enmity was based on a competitive struggle for the means of survival.

The bloodshed in the Balkans was similar, one of feared enemies competing in an enclosed and limited space. Fear and anger went hand in hand. The Palestinian/Israeli conflict can be structured in this way. But not Al Qaeda. Territory is not its goal. Ideology is. And envy, not fear, is the emotion that dictates its selection of an enemy.

Nevertheless, whether the battle is over ideology or territory, the real enemy is always the one within. The real mortification is one's own sense of personal inadequacy and failure. The hated communities are psychological displacements. For members of Al Qaeda and other anti-Americans, that displacement is dictated by envy. Neither the Jews nor the Americans threaten the religious belief of Islam. At least not by direct evangelical expansionism. The threat to Islamic communities is from the seductive image of a different life visualized through the extended perception of such modern technologies as international television, movies, CDs, DVDs, and particularly the Internet.

The United States is hated, not for the evil it has inflicted, but for its envied achievements, its seductive way of life. Anger is a response to the negative aspects of a culture; envy is a response to the positive. And who better to envy than the United States. The jihad may have been initiated by the mullahs out of their rejection of modernity, which they view as sacrilegious. But the masses have an authentic craving for the comforts and decencies of modern society. Only those with access to electricity romanticize the candle. Iran may have seceded from the modern world under the repressive regime of the mullahs, but Iranian antimodernism barely lasted one generation, even under the constrictive regime of a totalitarian theocracy.

Still, neither evangelical fervor nor envy can sustain a state of hatred. Hatred at its base is always a rationalization. It is a displacement to an identifiable other as the source of our personal miseries. Hatred is a disease, a social disease. And it is highly contagious.

I have heard many say, in defense of Palestinian hatred, that after generations of being kept in squalid refugee camps by their own people, becoming increasingly aware of a different and superior standard of living available to others, feeling frustrated and humiliated by the exercise of Israeli power, Palestinians are "entitled" to their hatred. This is one of the sad misunderstandings of the nature of hatred. Hatred is not entitlement like health care. It is a disease like tuberculosis. It may infect others, but it inevitably destroys the hater, diminishing his humanity and perverting the purpose and promise of life itself. No one is entitled to hatred any more than he is entitled to cancer.

In recent times the civilized European communities and the United Nations have honed their skills at detecting injustice by focusing on "American imperialism" and the "Israeli occupation." As I do not take any human rights violations lightly, I pay attention to their charges. Still, I am amazed by their peculiar insensitivity—one might say blindness—to the heinous crimes and atrocities committed on the African continent. Their umbrage threshold is very high when dealing with the slavery, abuse of women, child labor, even genocide that are endemic there. Whether this disparity of response is political correctness operating in concert with latent hostility to the privileged populations, or a reverse manifestation of racism that perceives barbarity as a more natural and permissible aspect of black and Arab cultures, I am not sure.

The hand-wringing in the United Nations and the press in Europe over the victims of American and Israeli acts of "genocide" in Afghanistan or the West Bank have so occupied the debates of the world community that the unspeakable war of true genocide in Sudan goes relatively unattended. The people of the Sudan live and starve in makeshift refugee camps in the shadows that lie beyond the astigmatic vision of the world bureaucracies. We can not afford the luxury of standing by. There are no more "local" problems in the area of hatred. We must heed the warning of Nelly Sachs:

> You onlookers
> Whose eyes watched the killing.
> As one feels a stare at one's back
> You feel on your bodies
> The glances of the dead.
>
> How many dying eyes will look at you
> When you pluck a violet from its hiding place?
> How many hands be raised in supplication
> In the twisted martyr-like branches
> Of old oaks?
> How much memory grows in the blood
> Of the evening sun?*

---

*Nelly Sachs, *O The Chimneys*, trans. Ruth and Matthew Mead (New York: Farrar, Straus and Giroux, 1967), p. 19.

14

CONFRONTING HATRED HEAD-ON

Whether through the special creation of God or a radical evolutionary adaptation, we human beings are unparalleled in the world of animals. That gift of freedom is the defining attribute of our distinctiveness. It is the underpinning of both human glory and human agony. It defines our way of life. The gift of freedom demands responsibility. Responsibility justifies moral condemnation and punishment. With knowledge comes good and evil, imagination and dread, anticipation and despair, creation and destruction. This combination of knowledge and freedom—freedom of action and responsibility—creates the moral universe.

The intellectual and creative use of knowledge—the foundation of our intelligence and imagination—has liberated most of us from spending our days absorbed in the struggle simply to stay alive. Through knowledge we have woven an elaborate cultural tapestry that defines modern existence beyond mere grubbing for survival. Through the exercise of freedom we have suffered unaccountable pain, but we have been able to lift ourselves out of the caves to traverse the very heavens.

But with our special knowledge we know how perilous that existence is. We know that however carefully we protect ourselves from predator or disease, death awaits us all. Animals fear the predator, but they do not know death. They cannot experience the human agony caused by the certitude of our own death. Cautious or not, lucky or not, privileged or deprived, we all die and the world goes on without us.

Many psychologists place the knowledge of death—and our need to live with this dreadful burden—at the forefront of our lives. How can something so central, so pivotal, to our own personal world—our self—be but an ephemeral and passing phenomenon? How can we be *disposable?* Such a narcissistic injury, such a blow to our own inflated self-worth, is simply not allowable. Since our own knowledge has brought us to the brink of this abyss, perhaps our imagination and intelligence can keep us from falling in.

The psychological term for closing your eyes to a reality is "denial." Ernest Becker, in his book *The Denial of Death,** viewed the world of neuroses as an elaborate means to disavow our own death. Many of the irrational anxieties that plague our existence he explains as mere displacements from the transcendent terror of our own inevitable end. Freud postulated the human invention of religion, with its promise of eternal life, as the ultimate denial of death. Freud saw religion as a human illusion designed to comfort us in the existential world of vulnerability and anxiety that we occupy.† The promise of the form of immortality known as an afterlife may be seen as an elaborate structure

---

*Ernest Becker, *The Denial of Death* (New York: Free Press, 1973).

†Sigmund Freud, *The Future of an Illusion*, 1927, 21:3.

to support the denial of death. The martyr trades the irrelevancy of a temporal and degraded life on earth for a permanent position at the side of God through eternity. The paradox is that except for the occasional martyr, most of us—including believers—cling tenaciously to life and try to protect ourselves against the terrors known and unknown that threaten us.

Known terrors are always more bearable than the dread of the unknown. What is knowable may be controllable. We use anticipation to protect ourselves by making contingency plans in advance of the impending disasters. When the reservoirs are dangerously low, we restrict water consumption. We store the bountiful harvests in anticipation of droughts, thus preventing famines. We arm ourselves in the presence of the predator; secure food supplies and stake out territories that supply them; protect ourselves from the elements; and in this modern age of medicine, take care of our health. Above all, we plan and anticipate. But there is no way that we can prepare our psyche to accept the unknown and unknowable. We, therefore, find means of rationalizing the unknowable.

The greatest perceived threat is always the unknowable one, which is epitomized by one of the earliest fears of childhood—fear of the dark. Even this fear represents a reparative step. It defines a way out. If that which one fears is literally "the dark," one can always turn on the light. With the intellectual and metaphoric darkness, we need symbolic candles. The evolution of the varying symptoms of neurosis, as described in Chapter 7, can all be explained in terms of controlling the unknowable by adding light and understanding. Neurotic behavior can be viewed as an attempt to control an existential, or free-floating, anxiety through various displacements and rationalizations.

All of us have felt anxious, as distinguished from worried. We worry about events. We are anxious about what we do not know. But for most of us, the anxiety we occasionally experience is similar to the temporary feelings of depression that we endure. We know that this vague anxiety—extending in severity from unease to dread—will pass. With some people, the anxiety will not pass. This is the state we psychiatrists refer to as an "anxiety neurosis." Such patients are forced to use the reparative devices of neurotic symptoms to help limit their anxiety. The phobic *avoids* the source of his anxiety; he decides that an animal is the true source of his fear and he stays away from that animal. The obsessive *eliminates* the source of his anxiety; if every aspect of life is managed and controlled, there can be no surprises, and thus there will be no uncontrollable events. The delusional *explains* it; that which seems threatening is really a part of a grand design to exalt rather than to reduce one. But all neurotic repairs eventually fail, as reality inevitably breaks through, necessitating newer distortions and displacements.

Hatred can be understood in the language of repair and symptoms. Hatred is a neurotic attachment to a self-created enemy that has been designed to rationalize the anxiety and torment of a demeaning existence. It is a defense against the hopelessness of despair. Hate-driven people live in the distorted world of their own perceptions. Normal people also live in the perceived world rather than the actual one, but saying that both the bigoted hater's perceptions and the normal person's perceptions are subjective does not eliminate the real distinction between those perceptions. It does not morally equate the hater with us. Hatred is their disease at this point, and we normal people must protect ourselves against it. To do so we must appreciate its complexities.

Hatred must not be perceived as a mere extension of the transient feelings of rage that we all have experienced. It is an emotion, but beyond that, it is also a psychological state that defines the self in terms of a relationship with an enemy. Hatred can be seen as being structured very similarly to love. However, the opposing feelings that underlie the two emotions make love an enriching and expansive experience, while hatred is a constricting and destructive venom. One can compare hatred and love:

1. Both are supported by powerful feelings, but both encompass more than feeling in their definitions. They are not simply emotions like rage, fear, guilt, or shame.
2. Both require a passionate attachment that must endure over a significant time.
3. Both require an object of their attachments. In a love relationship, the attachment is generally to an individual and the object is invariably idealized; in hatred the object of fixation is usually to a group and the object population is demonized.
4. Those who love or hate are obsessed with the objects of their emotional states and insist on sharing their lives with them.
5. Finally, both hatred and love involve an often dangerous infatuation—"a foolish, unreasoning, or extravagant passion"—and that can lead to disastrous action.

In neither hatred nor love is the object of their attachment, the obsessive focus of their passion, all that the individual makes it out to be. It is not surprising that, as William Congreve wrote, "love to hatred turned" is such a familiar story. All that is required is a shift in the emotion. Everything else is in place.

The fact that hatred is formed and structured like a neurosis does not mean that we ought to grant to hatred the exculpation afforded the sick. Antisocial behavior must be governed and controlled. To do that we insist on autonomy and responsibility. Unless you are truly insane, the presence or absence of mental illness has little relevance in the law. As Oliver Wendell Holmes said, "Men who are not insane nor idiotic [are expected] to control their evil passions or violent tempers or brutal instincts, and if they do not do so, it is their own fault."* The sardonic statement of the judge in Samuel Butler's *Erewhon* highlights the central position that responsibility holds in the social contract:

> You may say that it is not your fault. The answer is ready enough at hand, and it amounts to this—that if you had been born of healthy and well-to-do parents, and been well taken care of when you were a child, you would never have offended against the laws of your country, nor found yourself in your present disgraceful positions. If you tell me that you had no hand in your parentage and education, and that it is therefore unjust to lay these things to your charge, I answer that whether your being in a consumption [tuberculosis] is your fault or no, it is a fault in you, and it is my duty to see that against such faults as this the commonwealth shall be protected. You may say that it is your misfortune to be criminal; I answer that it is your crime to be unfortunate.†

Those of us who have never experienced the cold and continuing passion of hatred can never truly understand that which exists in the hearts of the haters. We do not know how "they feel when . . ." And for that we must be grateful. But to limit the reach of hatred, we must try to understand it. There *is* such a thing as evil; there is such a thing as paranoid displacement; there is such a thing as a culture of hatred. And it is with the last-named that the danger is compounded.

Generalized theories of violence and hatred often prove vulnerable because they seek a common internal dynamic that

---

*As quoted in Abraham Goldstein, *The Insanity Defense* (New Haven: Yale University Press, 1967), p. 192.

†Samuel Butler, *Erewhon* (New York: New American Library, 1960), pp. 93–94.

drives all haters. That problem almost destroyed psychoanalysis. Freud established his theory of neurosis built on unconscious drives and defenses against them. He postulated that dynamic forces from the patient's past determined his neurotic fate. Then Freud and his followers assumed they could find common patterns in all who suffered a similar neurosis. This ushered in the silly season of dynamic speculation that sought universal and overarching causes. Only later would psychoanalysts recognize that it was not a common drive or common past that determined the nature of a phobia, for example, but a common defense. The same is true of hatred.

Even the best of researchers continues to be beguiled into looking for universal causes for sociological behavior. Richard Rhodes, in his admirable book *Masters of Death*,* struggled in a similar fashion to find some common bonds that would link the Nazi SS murderers, in hopes of introducing some dynamic, regardless of how demented, that might explain the killings. But these people do not share a psychological unity or a basic dynamic. They are not a universe of like-minded people. Each of them is playing out his own scenario of misery and rage determined by his unique history.

Similarly, the profilers and other self-appointed predictors of human behavior patterns do a disservice to the complexity of human motivation by their generalizations. They inevitably describe the unknown terrorist in the image of his predecessor, and in the process often lead law enforcement down a garden path, as in the disastrous effort to find "the white man in a white van" in the search for the sniper killers in the Washington, D.C., area in the fall of 2002.

---

*Richard Rhodes, *Masters of Death: The SS-Einsatzgruppen and the Invention of the Holocaust* (New York: Knopf, 2002).

There are as many variations of psychodynamics leading to hatred as we find in neurotic patients. Each, neurotic and hater, takes the building blocks—his unconscious or conscious feelings of terror, deprivation, impotence, humiliation, and frustrated rage—and constructs a setting for hatred. Each one will search for direction and outlet for his misery that exonerates himself. He will build a scenario of persecution by utilizing whatever leads are at hand. He will invent an enemy. He may exploit individual scapegoats: blacks, Jews, abortionists, gays. He may discover a previously designed enemy supplied to him by groups with consonant concerns—safeguarding the environment, protecting animals, preserving racial purity.

The deranged individual has a limited capacity to wreak havoc. The psychotic is too disorganized to do much more than go on a shooting spree. As tragic as that is, it has relatively limited long-range consequences for society at large. The psychopath also has limits set on his actions. It is with the group—the culture of hatred—that monstrous evil can be unleashed. When the psychotic or paranoid is a despotic leader, like Idi Amin, with absolute authority over his nation, individual despair and resentment may be united under the banner of the leader's insane vision. When everyday bias is supported and legitimated by religion or nationalism, the passions of ordinary malcontents will be intensified and focused, allowing a community of hatred to emerge. The conditions necessary to support mass murder and genocide are now set.

A collection of haters is generally a ragtag assembly of individuals until a powerful authority, such as a political or religious leader, provides them with a common enemy. This paranoid leadership gives shape to the group by naming an enemy, by granting legitimacy and respectability to the hatred of that enemy through its authority, and by mobilizing the disorganized group into a killing culture. The aggregate becomes a mob, a troop, or an army, brought together by the shared enemy, which has been selected and offered up to them by the paranoid political state or the fanatic religious leaders. The common bond of hatred is the common enemy. The culture of hatred is the primary threat. We are right to treat Al Qaeda with deadly seriousness. We are right to view Saddam Hussein and the other despots of the world as potential Hitlers.

It is a sad truth that religious leaders often create a forum for the dissemination of hatred. We are told that the Muslim faith is one of tolerance. But what is the Muslim faith? And who articulates it? The mullahs are no more united than the Christian or Jewish theologians. Who speaks for Christ? The Roman Catholic church, the Southern Baptists, the Christian Militia? The same condition exists in the disparate worlds of Islam. Each mullah becomes a prophet for his own people. In our time, however, only the radical Islamists have captured the attention of media. We are experiencing the extensive influence of the Wahhabi faction over modern Islam, where every infidel is the hated enemy.*

The fanatic and xenophobic Wahhabi sect of Islam has been given legitimacy and financial support through the shortsightedness and recklessness of the leaders of Saudi Arabia. The Wahhabi disseminate their hatred and intolerance everywhere in the Muslim world through the activities of irresponsible mullahs, and with the money supplied them by feckless Arab political leaders, who ought to be held responsible. Their military arm is Al Qaeda. And they speak only of hatred and holy war.

As recently as the summer of 2002 the *New York Times* reported an interview in which a professor of Islamic law explained to a visiting reporter: "Well, of course I hate you because you are

---

*For a recent, detailed, and frightening indictment of Wahhabism, see Stephen Schwartz, *The Two Faces of Islam: The House of Saud from Tradition to Terror* (New York: Doubleday, 2002).

Christian, but that doesn't mean I want to kill you."* Well, the professor may not wish to kill the reporter, but the students he instills with his theological justifications of hatred may have different ideas about the proper expressions of hatred. If the theocratic dictators who dominate the oppressed minorities in Saudi Arabia and the other "moderate" Arab states think they can control the mass frenzy that they are either encouraging or tolerating, they profoundly misread human nature and the role that hatred can play.

We live in a time in which cultures of hatred exist predominantly in the Muslim world. But there are undoubtedly paranoid cultures in other areas, Africa, for example, where their effects are as yet so local and self-contained that they have not impinged on the consciousness of the larger world. It would be wise to direct some attention to these areas before the fact; to deal with the misery and frustration that are waiting to be molded into hatred before we are forced to. Once a culture of hatred has been firmly established, we are left with only the limited choices of disarming, diffusing, or destroying it.

I have tried to attend to the nature of hatred out of a feeling that a clearer understanding of its qualities can guide us in understanding its causes. The roots of hatred are buried under a surface of normalcy that obscures their depths and entanglements. They must be exposed and analyzed. I view a psychological analysis of hatred as a prerequisite, not an alternative, to investigating the social conditions that encourage its emergence; the economic aspects that cultivate it; the political and religious institutions that exploit it. Only with the knowledge of what hatred is can we uncover the conditions that nurture it.

A sense of deprivation has psychic roots independent of

---

*Neil MacFarquhar, "A Few Saudis Defy a Rigid Islam to Debate Their Own Intolerance," *New York Times*, July 12, 2002, p. A6.

poverty and want. We cannot control each individual's developmental background, and we do not need to. The isolated and individual hater can cause profound misery, but only to a limited few. The greater danger will always lie with those who would cynically manipulate and exploit such misery, those who would organize and encourage hatred for their political ends. We must attend to them, the preachers and organizers of hatred. We had a moral obligation to do so with the rise of Nazism. We didn't care enough then. Perhaps we do now.

The moral world is the preserve of mankind. We must cultivate it. In the end, the search for the heart of evil, the "unholy grail" as Walker Percy called it, may be as elusive as the search for the Holy Grail, but it is the quest that defines our humanity.

ACKNOWLEDGMENTS

Someone has to do the dirty work of reading an unkempt first draft. This is best hidden from all but the most forgiving. My brother, Dr. Sheldon Gaylin, also a psychiatrist, undertook this task and in the process managed to encourage and direct my progress. Further along, my sister-in-law, Rita Gaylin, offered the kind of detailed critique that only an avid reader and natural editor could supply. I am indebted to both of them. By then I was ready for a professional.

My long-time agent and friend Owen Laster once again proved his abilities by directing me to my current editor, Kate Darnton. Critical yet supportive, gentle but persistent, she applied her youthful enthusiasm and considerable talents to the task of improving this manuscript. She is a delight to work with.

With each new book, the task of "acknowledging" my wife's contributions to my work becomes more difficult. Time and love have eroded those separate identities—the her and me—that we first brought to our young relationship, leaving in its place a stubborn and persistent thing called "us".

INDEX

Communities of haters (*continued*)
  characteristics of, 218–224
  versus cultures of hatred,
    195–196, 214
  joined by religion, 224–235
Competition, 68–70
Congreve, William, 241
Conspiracy theory, 115–116
Crane, Stephen, 143n
Crime and Insanity in England, 95
Crime of Punishment, The, 9n
Criminal behavior
  and crimes of passion, 59
  and hate crimes, 8–9, 26–27,
    27–28, 138–139, 141, 200–201
  mental illness as defense for,
    9–13, 84–88, 95, 242
  and moral relativism, 8–9, 13,
    18–19, 84–88
  and paranoia, 112–113
  as a psychological disorder,
    14–15, 18–19
  and psychosis, 130–139, 145
  by radical single-issue activists,
    190–191
  and schizophrenia, 131–139
  See also Terrorists
Cultural differences
  and culture of hatred versus
    culture of haters, 195–196,
    214
  in early civilizations, 180–182
  in family values, 197–198
  generalizing, 197–199, 217
  and group identities, 104–105,
    163–164, 192
  and identification, 161–162
  and moral relativism, 199,
    234–235

and political correctness,
  234–235
in privacy, 111
and proximal identification,
  167–171

Death
  of children, 1–2, 5
  denial of, 238–239
  knowledge of, 238
  romanticizing, 5–6
Delusional Disorder, 122n
Delusions
  and anxiety, 123–124
  defining, 122–123
  versus hallucinations, 122–123
  in paranoia, 115
  in psychosis, 122–130
  and shame and guilt, 124–125
Denial, 238–239
Denial of Death, The, 238
Dennison, William, 190
Depression, 68–69, 123, 240
  in childhood, 155
Deprivation, 46–48, 70–71,
  246–247
  and envy, 66, 221–224
  and paranoia, 116–119
  and religion, 173–174
Dickens, Charles, 64, 151
Displacement, 100–101
Dostoyevsky, Fyodor, 78n
Downward identification, 164–167
Drowned and the Saved, The, 199n
Dugdale, Richard L., 144
Dunstan, Colin George, 137–138

Early Arab trauma, 85–86
Earth First Journal, 189

INDEX

and social rebellion, 49–51
and victim populations,
203–204
in youth, 6–7
Helder, Cameron, 133–134
Helder, Lucas John, 133–135, 145
Helplessness, 66–67
Herrin, Richard, 11–12
Hertz, J. H., 64n
Hilberg, Raul, 27, 200n
Hitler, Adolf, 13, 15, 18, 27, 105, 113,
145, 211, 212
Hitler's Willing Executioners, 113
Holmes, Oliver Wendell, 241–242
Holocaust, the, 1–3, 14, 15, 27, 28,
77, 90, 146–147, 177n, 190,
195, 200, 206–207, 230, 243.
See also Jews; Nazi Germany
Homosexuality, 126–129
Human behavior
and attitudes toward death, 5
caring, 79
in competition, 68–70
in contrast to animal behavior,
3–4, 37–40, 91–93, 169–170,
237–238
controlled by civilization and
community, 78–80, 82–83,
241–242
in depression, 68–69
diversity of, 76–77
effect of emotions on, 20–29,
33–34
and the fight or flight response,
39, 42–43
and free will, 81–82, 87–88,
237–238
Freudian analysis of, 81–84
and genetics, 151–152, 196

and group identities, 104–105,
118–119, 144
and humiliation, 44, 53, 59–62,
113–114, 156
and individual perception, 83
influence of life history on, 13
as inherently evil, 77–78
irrationality of, 79–80, 196
and mental illness, 9–13, 84–88,
95
and moral relativism, 8–9, 13,
18–19, 84–88, 199, 234–235
motivated by religion, 156–157,
227–229
and pecking orders, 43
profiling, 243
rationality of, 81
and romanticizing insanity, 87
and romanticizing violence, 5–6
See also Mental illness; Normal
human behavior
Hume, David, 168–169
Humiliation, 44, 53, 59–62,
113–114, 156
in psychosis, 128–129
Hussein, Saddam, 245
Hutu-Tutsi conflicts, 183–184
Hysteria, 96–97, 99, 126

Ideas of reference, 115
Identity
and discovering the self,
153–158
and downward identification,
164–167
and group identification,
104–105, 118–119, 144,
163–164, 170, 244–245
and modeling behavior, 158–160

INDEX

MacFarquhar, Neil, 246n
Manipulation, 53–54
Marxism, 47, 105, 151–152, 174n
Masters of Death, 91n, 243
Maternal instincts, 166–167
McVeigh, Timothy, 138, 145
Meaning of Despair, The, 33n
Mein Kampf, 211
Memoirs of a Neurotic, 125
Men
  women's betrayal of, 53–54
  and fear, 46
Menninger, Karl, 9n, 13
Mental illness
  assessing, 89–90
  as defense for pathological
    behavior, 9–13, 84–88, 242
  defense mechanisms of,
    100–101
  and displacement, 100–101
  Freudian analysis of, 96–106
  and group identities, 104–105
  and hysteria, 96–97, 99, 126
  Libido theory of, 98–99, 102
  and scapegoating, 100, 174–179
  scientific understanding of,
    95–98
  societal attitudes toward, 95–96
  of suicide bombers, 3, 6–7,
    75–76, 157, 166, 196
  symptoms of, 90–91, 100–103
  See also Abnormal human
    behavior; Paranoia
Middle class, American
  feelings of betrayal among,
    51–54
  traditional values, 49–51
Modeling, 158–160
Molière, Jean-Baptiste, 64

Moral relativism, 8–9, 13, 18–19,
  84–88, 199, 234–235
Morris, Desmond, 78n
Mosser, Thomas, 189
Munro, Alistair, 122n
Murder
  and black rage, 84–85
  bystanders to, 27–28
  of children, 1–2, 5, 85
  of gays, 8
  of Jews, 1–3, 27, 90, 146–147
  of women, 1–2, 11
  by youths, 6–7, 11–12
Murray, Gilbert, 190
Muslims. *See* Islam
Myth of Mental Illness, The, 87

Nanook of the North, 47
Narcissism, 114–115
Nasar, Sylvia, 125
Nash, John Forbes, Jr., 125, 126, 132
Nation, 8
Nature of Prejudice, The, 35, 36n,
  207, 220n
Nazi Germany
  dehumanizing Jews in, 210–211
  demonizing Jews in, 209–210
  leadership in, 211–213
  paranoia in, 211–212, 230
  and traditions of anti-Semitism
    in Europe, 208–209, 214–215
  See also Holocaust, the
Negativism, 113
Neighbors, 2
New Yorker, The, 177n
New York Times, 6, 7, 10n, 133n,
  138, 162n, 189, 245, 246n
Normal human behavior
  controlled by civilization, 78–80

257

PUBLICAFFAIRS is a publishing house founded in 1997. It is a tribute to the standards, values, and flair of three persons who have served as mentors to countless reporters, writers, editors, and book people of all kinds, including me.

I. F. STONE, proprietor of *I. F. Stone's Weekly*, combined a commitment to the First Amendment with entrepreneurial zeal and reporting skill and became one of the great independent journalists in American history. At the age of eighty, Izzy published *The Trial of Socrates*, which was a national bestseller. He wrote the book after he taught himself ancient Greek.

BENJAMIN C. BRADLEE was for nearly thirty years the charismatic editorial leader of *The Washington Post*. It was Ben who gave the *Post* the range and courage to pursue such historic issues as Watergate. He supported his reporters with a tenacity that made them fearless, and it is no accident that so many became authors of influential, best-selling books.

ROBERT L. BERNSTEIN, the chief executive of Random House for more than a quarter century, guided one of the nation's premier publishing houses. Bob was personally responsible for many books of political dissent and argument that challenged tyranny around the globe. He is also the founder and was the longtime chair of Human Rights Watch, one of the most respected human rights organizations in the world.

.   .   .

For fifty years, the banner of Public Affairs Press was carried by its owner Morris B. Schnapper, who published Gandhi, Nasser, Toynbee, Truman, and about 1,500 other authors. In 1983 Schnapper was described by *The Washington Post* as "a redoubtable gadfly." His legacy will endure in the books to come.

Peter Osnos, *Publisher*